Aunt Sue and Uncle Wes,

Thank you for always being such a great support to us. We love you deeply.

In such a time as this,

Claus C. Stone

12/31/10

DEFEATING FEAR

DEFEATING FEAR

*Proven Biblical
Strategies to
Fight Fear
and Win*

Carrie C. Stone

COURAGE HOUSE
PUBLISHING

Courage House Publishing
P.O. Box 1531
Anacortes, WA 98221

ISBN# 978-1-4507-4207-8

Unless otherwise indicated, Scripture references are taken from the New International
Version® of the Holy Bible. Copyright © 1973, 1978, 1984 by International Bible
Society. Used by permission of Zondervan Publishing House. Scripture quotations
marked AMP are from the Amplified Version of the Bible. Old Testament copyright
© 1964, 1987 by the Zondervan Corporation. The Amplified New Testament
copyright © 1954, 1958, 1897 by the Lockman Foundation. Used by permission.
Scripture quotations marked NKJV are from the New King James Version of the Bible.
Copyright © 1979, 1980, 1982 by Thomas Nelson, Inc., publishers. Used by
permission. Scripture quotations marked NLT are from the New Living Translation
Version of the Bible. Copyright © 1996, 2004 by Tyndale Charitable Trust.
Used by permission of Tyndale House Publishing. Used by permission. Scripture
quotations marked NASB are from the New American Standard Bible Version of the
Bible. Copyright © 1960, 1962, 1968, 1971, 1973, 1975, 1977, 1995 by
The Lockman Foundation. Used by permission.

Cover Design: Julie Riley, j.riley creative LLC
Cover Photo: Renee Bergeron, Little Earthling Photography
Interior Design: Julie Riley, j.riley creative LLC

Printed in the United States of America

COURAGE HOUSE
PUBLISHING

CONTENTS

DEDICATION

I dedicate this book to my sister, Elizabeth Ann Chillas
(11/30/66 – 12/22/92), who faced her fears and accomplished
her destiny in a life that ended much too soon. She always was and
continues to be a great source of hope and inspiration to me
and to all who were blessed enough to know her.

ACKNOWLEDGEMENTS

Thank you to the entire Marching Though Culpeper prayer team. You came into my life at just the right time. Your commitment to pray for me each week made a greater difference than any of you could know.

Thank you, Randi Zetting, for not only leading and rallying the intercessors, but for all of the long drives out to comfort me, the endless edits, the hours of analyzing Scriptures and the personal financial investment you made in supplying for all of my needs! You are a treasure of great worth to me.

Special thanks go out to Mandy Holden (a.k.a. My Mandy, or Angel Girl). You helped me keep everything going while also debating the issues I needed to work out, praying and just making me smile. You are a shining example of a warrior who allows nothing to hold you back. I am so proud to know you and am so grateful I have had the privilege of loving you.

Virginia Morton, what can I say? Everyone needs one person in their lives who believes in them not just in words, but in deeds. You have been that person to me. Thank you for the heartfelt prayers, the endless encouragement, the FOUR edits, and for the final kick in the pants I needed to make this happen. You are a gem!

Thanks to Judi Reid for not only seeing something in me, but for tangibly helping me to live out my destiny in a very detailed way! You have become a valued friend to me.

To Diana Morse for always reminding me of who I am first – a child of God, a wife to Rod and a mother to the two greatest kids in the world. You are my stabilizer and a constant strength to me.

Huge thanks must go out to Mark and Lynn Cross and Dave and Sue Schwab not just for your encouraging friendships, but for generously allowing me to use your vacation homes to escape and write. Those times of removal from the world brought about most of the pages of this book.

Thanks to Julie Riley for your great cover and interior work, to Renee Bergeron for the cover picture, to Pastor Dax Swanson for always challenging me, to Jodi Whisenhunt for stretching yourself to do my final edit, and to all of the mighty warriors I am blessed to meet along the way who inspired the pages of this book.

A thank you would not be sufficient for my two babies, Newell and Olivia. You are my fearless ones. You remind me every day who I am and why I do what I do. Thank you for always encouraging me to live out my destiny even when it costs you something. You inspire me and motivate me to want to be better. I love you more than life!

To my beloved, Saint Rod, with whom I am well pleased. I owe you everything. You are my biggest fan, my greatest encourager, my best friend, and the love of my life. Thank you for giving me the freedom to be all God created me to be, for believing in me when I didn't believe in myself, for wiping my tears, for picking me up off the floor in those painful moments, for loving me more when I was broken, for picking up my slack when I was in the throes of writing, and for just being so incredibly wonderful. I am a better person because I know you. I more than love you!!

And finally, to my precious Creator, thank you for trusting me with this responsibility. My greatest fear is that I would ever let you down. Thank you for the times of pruning which brought forth great fruit. Thank You for never leaving me and for truly supplying all of my needs. You are an awesome God, and I am honored to serve and worship You with my life.

PREFACE

"T'was Grace that taught...my heart to fear.
And Grace, my fears relieved. How precious did that Grace appear...
the hour I first believed.

"I thank Thee, likewise, for the subsequent month, when we
(aboard ship) expected to be starved, or reduced to feed upon one another
and had it not been for this protected season of distress, my first
impressions might have worn off, but Thou fixed and increased them, so
that by the time we arrived in Ireland, I was no longer an infidel. Not
one of my fellow sufferers was affected as I was. Well I might say with
wonder and gratitude, Why me, O Lord, Why me?"
John Newton

I had suffered from fear throughout my life, but had learned to be victorious in spite of it. Through it all, I relied on Christ to overcome. I never imagined that I needed any more battles with fear to fill the pages of this book. And yet, during the writing, I walked through the dark and lonely valleys of impending foreclosure and career upheaval.

From the writing of the very first words, fears attempted to overtake me: the fear of failure, the fear of rejection, the fear of not completing the book, and the loss of income during the writing. Fear overwhelmed me as my emotions ran high, and I questioned everything I wrote. Finally, after several days of heated spiritual battle, I felt weakened to the point of wanting to quit. Scared and lonely, I knew with certainty I was not the person for this task. I began to wonder, "Is this worth the effort?" Finally, in tears and submitted before God, I cried out "Lord, why did you choose me to write about fear? **Why me?** I am not worthy." Finally, in the quietness of my spirit, the answer came. "You are not worthy, Carrie, but you are willing and obedient. That is all I ask of you."

So in willingness and obedience, I submit my life experiences through this book. My prayer is that God will use it to prevent you from drowning in the sea of desperation, desolation, and destruction caused by living a life of fear.

DEFEATING FEAR

INTRODUCTION

"No eye has seen, no ear has heard, no mind has conceived
what God has prepared for those who love Him"
I Corinthians 2:9

"It seemed impossible to leave the world before I had
brought forth all I was destined to do."
Ludwig Van Beethoven

Every once in a while I meet someone who claims to fear nothing. And I am reminded of the mighty men and women of God who appeared to be fearless. Yet when we read their words, we quickly learn they were far from fearless.

This reminds me of our Bahaman honeymoon experience. My husband and I decided to go on an acrylic submarine ride. As we boarded the large, plastic-like vessel, we laughed and sang, "We're going down in an acrylic submarine, an acrylic submarine, an acrylic submarine." In spite of being consumed with one another, we couldn't miss the hulk-sized professional football player who boarded with us. This huge guy looked fearless. I certainly did not want to annoy him in any way. But we watched the look of sheer terror transform his face, and then we quickly stopped singing and began to pray for this "fearless" one. This man faced men larger and scarier than himself every week for a living! Every time he stepped onto the football field, he risked injury, paralysis, and even death. Yet his fear of being in confined spaces caused him to shake, vomit, and cry. It turns out he was not so fearless after all.

None are fearless, and actually, fear can be a good thing because it makes you need God. Problems arise when it stops you from living out your purposes for Him. Far too many people allow fear to control them to the point that they never step out to accomplish their destinies. I admit allowing it to stop me from time to time and you probably do too. Maybe you haven't asked for the promotion out of fear of being turned down. Maybe the fear of losing your home keeps you awake at night, or fear about your job, your marriage, your child, or your hard-earned life savings consumes you. Or perhaps you greatly fear disappointing others, so you stay in a job you hate. Maybe your reluctance to make the phone calls, preach the sermon, discipline your child, stand up for your beliefs, or defend the helpless haunts you. Whether you are dealing with fear of man, fear of rejection, fear of failure, fear of loss, fear of death, fear of sickness, or any of the many destiny destroying fears, you have found the right book. Within these pages you will learn strategies for overcoming the paralysis of fear. Prepare to break shackles, escape the prison bars of fear, and claim the destiny God laid out for you before the beginning of time.

How is fear affecting your life right now? Is it holding you back from your dreams? Does it render you helpless and hopeless? Has it been lying, cheating, and berating you throughout your life? If you continue on this path, what legacy will you leave future generations? No matter your age, size, upbringing, social status, or color, you can impact the world by choosing to overcome the paralysis of fear and stepping into your God-ordained destiny.

Throughout the yearlong process of writing this book, I have poured out my heart and soul. I wrote every word as an act of obedience to God and to His calling on my life. By constantly battling the demon fear, I have tested every included exercise as have my clients and audiences. God inspired the action steps in Section Four prior to my women's group talk and these steps grew into the basis for this book. I placed them at the end of the book for a reason. Before going into battle for your destiny, you must better understand yourself and your enemy fear. The exercises and insights in Sections One and Two will help you do just that. In Section Three you will find the lives of three men God anointed and appointed for great works. Understanding the lives of these heroes will encourage and empower you. This knowledge and inspiration will prepare you to step onto the battlefield for your destiny and apply the action steps found in the final section.

I recommend that you keep your Bible handy as you read through *Defeating Fear*. The Word of God is your final authority. Make it a practice to question what you hear and read. The knowledge you gain by searching for truth within the Bible will strengthen your faith, weaken your fear and prepare you for victory. So search away.

As you read, be prepared for God to move mightily in your life. I pray that you will come face-to-face with the One who can free you from the paralysis of fear and propel you into a life you cannot even imagine. God's Word will take you to depths of understanding you didn't even know existed. Don't go alone – take someone with you. Share the exercises with others and discuss the principles laid out for you.

Lastly, expect God to speak to your spirit as you commit to overcoming the paralysis of fear. Expect Him to change your life because He will. As you walk in obedience to His leading, you will find peace and joy like you have never known. True victory is found by *Defeating Fear*!

DEFEATING FEAR

SECTION I

GETTING TO KNOW YOU

*"Do not be afraid, Daniel. Since the first day that you set your mind
to gain understanding and to humble yourself before your God,
your words were heard, and I have come in response to them."*
Daniel 10:12 (NLT)

*"Most people live and die with their music still un-played.
They never dare to try."*
Mary Kay Ash

We all like to get things. We like to get a good job, a new car, a
spouse, and lots of money. Sometimes just the getting of something
new makes it so special, but once the new car smell wears off, the
excitement of the new job or marriage disappears, or we grow accustomed to the higher income, we find ourselves wanting to get more.
God gifted King Solomon to be the wisest man of all time, and in
Proverbs 4:5 he instructs us to not get things, but instead to *"Get wisdom; get understanding."* Get is an action verb and this book promotes
taking action. As we get wisdom and understanding, we discover the
freedom to soar to previously impossible heights. In this book you will
learn to trample the darkness that has dissipated your light and step

confidently into the future that was laid out for you by God from the beginning of time.

To overcome the paralysis of fear, you must understand not only who you are, but Whose you are and why you are here. Otherwise, you will continuously fall back into old patterns and spend your life making prison breaks from fear only to be captured once again.

Take a journey with me as we heed King Solomon's advice. By getting understanding, wisdom, and knowledge, you will become empowered to expose and defeat the enemy who holds your promised future hostage.

Your power is in your purpose. You will find your purpose as you become educated in the subject of you.

SECTION I • GETTING TO KNOW YOU

1   Who You Are

*"For we are God's masterpiece. He has created us anew in Christ Jesus, so
we can do the good things he planned for us long ago."*
Ephesians 2:10 (NLT)

*"When we don't understand who we are, we don't experience the freedom
and fruitfulness which is intrinsic to our identity."*
Neil T. Anderson – The Bondage Breaker

KNOW YOURSELF

Life as we know it is constantly changing. Who we are and the
titles we hold seem to change as quickly as the green leaves of summer
turn to a brilliant array of fall color. From child to adult, from adult to
spouse, from spouse to parent and from parent to grandparent, life is
ever changing, ever expanding, ever confusing. It is no wonder that I
have so many people come to me questioning who *they* are.

As if life itself does not bring enough confusion with its barrage
of uncertainties, add to that a lifetime of instances where others have
been trying to tell you who you are. Maybe you are the bright one, the
talented one, the quiet one, the loud one, the smart one or the stupid
one. You may be the beauty queen, the football star, the fat one, the
skinny one, or the disabled one. These titles seem to stick with you as

you go through life. No matter what changes occur, the memory of the person others thought or said you were still seems to linger on.

There comes a time in life when you need to know for yourself who you are, not through the lenses of others, but through the lens of the person who ought to know you best—You.

You may be wondering what all of this has to do with fear, and to that question I say it has everything to do with fear. Fear takes root in your insecurities. Fear uses all of your weaknesses against you to keep you from your destiny. Sounds like a conspiracy, doesn't it? Well, it is! Fear is conspiring against you to bring you defeat, but when you understand who you are, you will have the ability to be who you are. Having knowledge of your identity will help to establish you in your purpose and it will give you the resolve to stand up when you want to fearfully shrink back.

My life, like yours, has had its ups and downs. From mountains to valleys, from life to near- death, and back again, this is the road we travel. Times of laughter are often followed by seasons of sorrow, and in my life, I have had much of both.

For me, it seemed that about the time I thought I knew who I was, something happened and my identity changed forever. I started life as a daughter to David and Dotti and a sister to Amy and Beth. Though no family is perfect, I had comfort in the fact that I knew who I was and where I belonged until that fateful day when I heard those words many of you have either heard or spoken yourself, "Mommy and Daddy just don't love each other anymore." In one nine word sentence my life was changed, along with my identity, forever.

These moments tend to do that, don't they? In the blink of an eye, the person you once knew is gone and in their place is someone you do not even recognize. All it takes is a call from the doctor with the dreaded news. Suddenly, your new title is "cancer patient." You hope to become a cancer survivor, but no matter what, you will never be the person you were before the phone rang. Or the one you were before you found the note. The one left behind by the same person who stood with you in front of God, your family, and your friends and vowed their eternal love. Now they are gone and with them they took the identity you had become accustomed to. Or maybe it is the identity you had before that awful day when you heard the knock at the door.

I remember that knock like it was yesterday. As I opened the door to find my stepfather standing there with a look on his face that could only mean bad news. The blast of cold air that came in with him was as chilling as the message he delivered. As the door closed behind him, the person I had been was shut out too. "Your sister is dead." Identity lost.

When I stood over my sister's body in the hospital, I remember becoming keenly aware that I would never be the same again. And suddenly, it was as if I had been transported in time to a long country road that had come to a fork. Which way to go? For the first time in my life I knew that I was an active participant in choosing my identity. I sensed that this experience would either destroy me or make me stronger. If I made no decision I would be subject to the random universe in which so many put their trust. As I felt the tug of the Holy Spirit, the choice became clear. I could not do this alone. Finally, I was ready to admit that I needed to purposefully change my identity. So, standing there over my sister's body, I gave my life to Jesus, and I have never been the same. With the death of one great love, a greater love was born. Identity found.

"WHO AM I?"

*"I pray also that the eyes of your heart may be enlightened in order
that you may know the hope to which he has called you,
the riches of his glorious inheritance in the saints, and his
incomparably great power for us who believe."*
Ephesians 1:18-19

*"You cannot perform in a manner inconsistent with
the way you see yourself."*
Zig Ziglar

You spent more on your anniversary dinner than you had planned, but you didn't mind. Twenty-five years deserved a celebration. Little did you know that as you looked longingly into the eyes of your beloved, your waiter gazed at your credit card through the lens of his cell phone camera, snapping pictures of his newfound love. Suddenly, your $200.00 dinner turned into a $2,000.00 expense which took two months to resolve. You became a victim of identity theft.

In this obvious attempt to rob you financially, you jumped to attention and took the steps necessary to fix the problem. You felt violated by the offense of a stranger. Your fury burned during the time it took to resolve the discrepancy with the credit card company. Yet for years the same thing has happened to you on a regular basis while you went about the daily routine of life. What makes this experience any different? How much of your identity have you lost by believing the lies others have told you about yourself?

If you have ever changed the way you think, dress, speak, or believe just to fit in, you have been a victim of identity theft. If you have ever made decisions based on what everyone else was doing even though you knew it was not right for you, you have been a victim of identity theft. It is time for you to turn off the bad commercial with the voiceover of a thug who has taken control of your future by usurping your identity and learn who you are.

Have you found your identity? Do you know beyond a shadow of a doubt who you are, or are you stuck in a life that others have laid out for you? In the movie, "Runaway Bride," Julia Roberts plays a character who has lost her identity. She goes from relationship to relationship trying to conform to someone else's vision of who she should be. In her confusion she lets others determine her likes and dislikes to the point where she has no idea about something as simple as how she likes her eggs. Can you relate? I've known people who have worked for years in jobs they hated because others thought they should. These people are not the exception, but the rule. I walked a very politically correct line for years because others told me to do so. What have you done? Coming to terms with who you are brings you freedom. In order to walk in the fullness of the life you were designed to live, you need to know yourself. For some this comes easily, but for others, well, we must learn the hard way.

IDENTITY CHECK

I have been known by others as a workaholic. I am an all-or-nothing person whether I am working or playing. When I became a career woman, my all went into making money. After marriage, my sickness of overworking was shoved aside because of a more serious disease. I had struggled with health issues for years, but overnight I had changed from a vibrant young bride to a sick, tired, and agitated mother. Then suddenly, after four years of being bedridden, I finally received an accurate diagnosis–Celiac Disease was destroying my immune system. Once I learned that my cure was simply to avoid all gluten products, I rose up, healthy and ready to face the world again. A year later, I was back in business. My life had become like a poorly produced Oliver Stone movie with its sudden bam-chuck-kong scene change. From black-and-white to color. I am sure you can relate. One day you are strong, the next you are weak. One day you are a successful business woman, the next you are a stay-at-home mommy. Our lives frequently get stuck in fast forward—from deadlines to diapers—from a home full of children to an empty nest. How can anyone keep up?

As we go from scene change to scene change, our titles may vary but the person inside doesn't always follow the screen play. With marriage, motherhood and a strong faith, I thought I would no longer battle the addiction to which I had once been a slave—workaholism. I thought I had control of my life. I thought I could handle all of the incredible pressure that comes with building a new business and still be the picture perfect mother. And therein lies the problem…I thought. Have you ever told God what He needed to do and how He needed to do it? I have too. I am sure you found as I did that He does not seem to follow your instructions very well. God's design is balanced. For balance, you must understand who you are.

THE ENCOUNTER

My family was sitting in the living room enjoying the fire while reading and playing games. I did what I always did: I worked. Like so many people today, I was searching and wandering aimlessly through life to find the balance I heard so many recommending. This particular evening, my desire to find balance was overtaken by my need to achieve. I was listening to an audio teaching when I heard a voice saying, "Who are you?" I shook my head and tried to concentrate on the message of the audio when I heard it again, "Who are you?" Well, I may be hardheaded sometimes, but this time I knew I needed to listen. I shut off the recording, pulled out a piece of paper and wrote in big letters at the top of the page, "Who Am I?"

Without over thinking, I began to list as quickly as they came to mind who I was. "I am a wife, a mother, a daughter, a friend, a Christian, an entrepreneur, a motivator, and a philanthropist." It was funny how quickly it came to me. I was thrilled to finally see in big black letters the reality of who I was. I began to read it aloud when I noticed that something just didn't seem right. I had written the eight things I could think of, and fifth on that list of eight things was Christian. Being a Christian is what causes me to be better at all of my other titles. It is that title which causes me to honor my father and my mother, to love and discipline my children, to adore and respect my husband, to cherish my friends at all times, to do business with integrity, to encourage and motivate others, and to give generously with no thought of anything in return. That title, the one taken too lightly by too many in our world today, should cause all of us to do things excellently. It should leave a lasting imprint on our lives and on the lives of others.

When you say you are a Christian, I hope you understand what you are saying. You are not making a simple religious statement; instead, at the depth of its meaning, you are saying as John did throughout the book of John that you are the one whom Jesus loves. You are loved by God. That is your true identity. Nothing can change it. No sin can separate you from this gracious gift of mercy. Isn't that amazing? Doesn't that just make you sit in awe of the One Who created you–the

One Who identifies you as the one He loves? When you look at the title of Christian from that perspective, it is hard to place it anywhere else but first on your list, isn't it?

When I changed the order of my titles, there was a peace that settled within my soul. I read the paper over and over. "I am a Christian, a wife, a mother, a daughter, a friend, an entrepreneur, a motivator, and a philanthropist." My identity was becoming clearer, and with it my vision was expanding.

For weeks I read the list over and over again until it was etched in my mind. I went to bed saying it and woke repeating it to myself. As it became embedded in my heart I began to see the importance of it. As I said earlier, when you know who you are, you have the ability to be who you are. Seeing this list in order of importance helped me to know where to place my priority. It became a constant reminder of what and who comes first. Your work is important, but not as important as your God, your spouse, and your kids. Your first mission field is in your home. I know it is easy to justify ignoring the mundane responsibilities of home life when there are so many important things to be done at the church or in your business, but you will never be able to go back and make up lost time to your family later. When you are ready, they may not be there. I have heard the justifications, but here is the truth. If what you want to do does not line up with the Word of God, it may look good and it may make sense by the world's standards, but that does not make it right by God's. Remember *"Where your heart is, there your treasure will be also"* (Matthew. 6:21).

GETTING THE HOUSE IN ORDER

My excitement was gaining intensity. This was the best business letter I had ever written. I was sure this was going to be the thing that would break open the flood gates of prosperity in my life. The excitement was so great, I shook as I typed. Everything was perfect. The thoughts were flowing. The ideas were pouring forth like a rushing river after the rain. The dam was ready to burst. Nothing could be better until…knock, knock, knock. The door slowly swung open, and there stood my precious little girl. Fresh up from her nap, her big, blue, groggy eyes peered over the top of the blankie I made her just three years earlier which was attached to her fingers perched perfectly in her mouth. Her cheeks were red and her hair was wet and matted to her head. With the innocence of an angel she looked up at me and said, "Snuggle, Mommy." Did she not know? Could she not see? I was on the verge of something great. I knew that if I stopped now it would all be lost. Just as I was about to impatiently let her know that she was interrupting, I saw it out of the corner of my eye—The List. Who am I? My heart broke with conviction as I looked into her sweaty little face. I grabbed my baby up in my arms, held her close and told her, "I always have time to snuggle you."

We both had our love tanks filled that afternoon as I kissed her fingers and her toes and squeezed her tight. It did not take long to give her what she needed. After what seemed only moments, she was off and running as she went to find her brother. I'd like to say that God blessed me that afternoon for doing the right thing by giving me an even better letter in exchange for my being so incredibly wonderful (just kidding), but He didn't. I was blessed that day, though, for walking in obedience. I had a moment with my little girl that I could never recreate. I built security in her that she will carry with her throughout her lifetime, and

I allowed a memory between a mother and a daughter to be born in the midst of the busyness of life. I have no regrets from that afternoon but I would have had I reacted the way I once did. Knowing who I am has allowed me to walk in the perfection of who I was created to be, and it will help you too.

Right now, take out a piece of paper, and at the top write, "Who Am I?" Then, without over analyzing, list your titles. Leave nothing out. You can always shorten the list later. Once you have completed that, put the titles in order of priority. Not your priority but God's.

I know this will be harder for some than for others, but please do not neglect this essential step in your journey. Understanding yourself is vital as you prepare to take down the giant called fear. As we head into the action steps to your freedom you will be glad you took the time to find out who you are. Your preparation for battle has begun.

Incidentally, if God isn't already at the top of your "Who Am I?" list, have no fear, by the end of the next chapter He will be.

SECTION I • GETTING TO KNOW YOU

2   Whose Are You

*"But if serving the Lord seems undesirable to you, then choose
for yourself this day whom you will serve..."*
Joshua 24:15

*"God is not what you imagine or what you think you understand.
If you understand you have failed."*
Saint Augustine

You could stop right here and find more success in your life simply
by knowing who you are. This knowledge will undoubtedly help you
to get ahead in the world. We have all observed countless people who
have accomplished great, worldly, wonderful things because they knew
who they were. Review any self-help program out there and you will
find that your identity is an essential part of your success. Of course,
much of that identity is found not in who you know yourself to be,
but in who you tell yourself you are. Although I am a firm believer in
speaking life and not death over oneself, I believe that anything that is
not founded on truth will prove to be its opposite—a lie. And whatever
is founded on a lie will die.

Have you been taught to visualize what you want? Were you told
to think on it? Dream about it? Speak it over yourself? Make a dream
board? These are things successful people do, right? And these are great

exercises if, and only if, you are thinking on, dreaming about, and speaking of the visions God has given you. I once heard a story of a precious little girl who loved to watch her mother plant flowers. One day, she decided that she too would dig and plant so that she could be like her Mommy. She took the prettiest stick she could find, looked for the ideal spot and lovingly planted her stick. This innocent one called out to her Daddy and said, "Look, Daddy, at my pretty flower." Her father praised her efforts even though he knew that no matter how much fertilizer or water his little girl applied to the soil, her stick would never be a beautiful flower. The same is true for you. If you attempt to grow the dreams of another, or to live out someone else's story, no matter what you do, your efforts will fail. You have a destiny and a purpose meant only for you. You will find that purpose, you will be able to take the steps to overcome the paralysis of fear, and you will accomplish your destiny when you can hear the still small voice of the Holy Spirit. Then you will see the vision God has placed before you. This will only happen if you know who you are in Him.

But you have an enemy lurking about who does not want you to know who you are in Christ. He wants you to know who you are in sin, in failures, and in weaknesses. He wants you to believe you can do everything on your own, because as long as he has you thinking that, you will be powerless. This foe knows that fear will take over when your eyes are focused on yourself instead of being focused on your God.

I am known for being a very black-and-white person. Grey is just not a color that has ever really suited me! So I am going to give it to you straight. You are going to serve somebody in your life. There is dark and there is light. There is right and there is wrong. And there comes a time when fence riding is just not fun anymore. The Bible says if you are not for God, you are against Him. So who will you choose? Will you be a fair weather follower or a sold out servant?

LEFT AT THE 50 YARD LINE

"Can two walk together, unless they are agreed?"
Amos 3:3 (NKJV)

The Super Bowl of 2000 started out to be a great one for me. We were living in Nashville, Tennessee, at the time, so having the Tennessee Titans make it to the big game was very exciting. Our team, the one we had rooted for all season, faced the Los Angeles Rams. The only thing I knew about the opposing team was that their quarterback was a Christian named Kurt Warner. That worried me.. My husband and I were visiting my family in Delaware at the time and I was very pregnant with our first child. I share all of this information with you for a reason, so stay with me. We started out strong in the first quarter, but every time Warner took the field the Rams slayed, filleted, and dismayed the Titans. It was embarrassing to watch, especially since everyone else in the room was rooting for the Rams except for us. Or so I thought it was us, until my husband, the man whose child I was carrying, who lived in Tennessee, who had supported the Titans all season, whom I had never even heard mention the L.A. Rams, not once, turned on me. He decided mid-game that his team was not good enough, so he started cheering for the opposing side. How can you do that, especially to your pregnant wife? How can you stop mid-game and switch teams? Where is your loyalty? All kidding aside, this is what we do in life, isn't it?

When we need help, when life is too hard, when we have nowhere else to turn, we turn to God. But when we want to do our own thing, when rebellion rises up within us, we turn against Him, and then blame Him when things go wrong. In the game of life, when circumstances are not going our way, we switch sides faster than you can say Super Bowl. This should not be the case for the person seeking victory. If you want to accomplish your goals in life, you must be sold out for them. If you want to have a strong marriage, you must be committed to it. And if you want to live a life of victory, one of joy, and one of peace, you must be devoted to God. His promises never fail. His truth never changes. His ways are perfect. If you want to slay the giant, you will not be able to straddle the fence. If you are one of the millions who have been seduced and drawn in by the lure of the self-centeredness of our secular Christianity, make a decision today to stop, to stand, to search, and to serve the One true God.

Do you know this God in an intimate way? Have you placed all of your hope in Him alone? Do you trust Him to lead you in the paths of righteousness? Do you recognize His voice, heed His calls, and walk in all of His ways? Are you sold out to His purposes and willing to die to your own? No matter how you answered these questions, prepare yourself now to know and love Him more.

THE BIOGRAPHY OF A SAVIOR

> *"Who is this King of Glory?*
> *The Lord strong and mighty,*
> *the Lord mighty in battle."*
> *Psalm 24:8*

Who is this God of Glory? Who is this Prince of Peace, this King of Kings, and this Lord of Lords? We sing our favorite worship songs at the top of our lungs; yet, do we really comprehend who He is? I think many times we see God as some sort of mystical being, but He is not mystical. He is not magical, He is not your personal genie, and He is not the universe or whatever you feel comfortable calling Him. He is outside of His creation. He is not politically correct. He does not plan to make everyone happy and feel good. He alone is God, the creator of the universe. The Maker and Creator of Heaven and Earth is His name.

The songs we sing speak of the greatness of our King, but do we believe the words that pour from our lips? Do they reach the depths of our soul with a resounding yes and amen? Do we have any concept of His greatness, an understanding of His grace and mercy, or a reverential awe and fear of His deity? Based on the evidence surrounding us today, I would say the answer is a resounding no.

MEET YOUR MAKER

If God were to write a resume, what would it look like? Talk about a Renaissance man, this guy has done it all. Can you imagine conducting an interview with Him? "Ah, so I see here God, that you created the world in six days. That's impressive. Then you established order so that all creation would prosper. That shows great ingenuity and leadership. You have been characterized as a strong disciplinarian. I am sure that does not always make you popular does it? Hmm, you destroyed the world because the people fell away from you. That seems a bit harsh, doesn't it? But then I see you restored it again. You call yourself a promise keeper, a dream giver, a protector, a rescuer, a rock, a shield, and a giver of life. My, is there anything you can't do?"

The paragraph above does not even begin to describe God's awesomeness. Look at the expanse of the universe. The God who created each of the billions of stars in the sky created you, and He knows every hair on your head. For some reason, Job understood this long before man had any sort of intelligent proof of creation. He spoke of God in awe when he declared, *"He is the Maker of the Bear and Orion, the Pleiades and the constellations of the south"* (Job 9:9). Job comprehended the greatness of his God, and he marveled at the fact that God knew him. Imagine the security he must have felt as he cried out to his Father, *"What is man that you make so much of him, that you give him so much attention, that you examine him every morning and test him every moment?"* (Job 7:17-18).

When we fix our eyes on God and His immensity, when we can step away from the mirror and see past our physical appearance to the spiritual power within us through Christ, then and only then, can we march boldly forward toward the destiny laid out for us by God before the beginning of time. When our eyes are on Him and His Word is implanted in our hearts, we will see, hear, and understand the vision of the future He prepared for us. But instead, we tell Him what He needs to do through us. When we understand how very small we are and how very big He is, then we can break forth, we can shine brightly in a dark world and we can accomplish His purpose for us. Oh, the glory of His name, the magnificence of His power, and the indescribable love He has for us.

He is terrifyingly holy, yet mysteriously compassionate. He is un-flinchingly faithful, yet unwaveringly just. He is unbound by physical-ity, time, and space. He is God. This knowledge of Him should cause us to live in the only fear we should allow to enter our lives and that is the fear of this almighty God of Israel. He is the Messiah, the Alpha and Omega, the Beginning and the End, the Author and Finisher of our faith, the Light of the World, Immanuel, the Great I AM.

Who is this King of Glory? Who is this Prince of Peace? He alone is the Author of your destiny. He alone deserves all of your praise. He alone has set His purpose for you in this life and in that purpose He will be glorified and your desires will be met. You cannot speak into being what He does not desire for you. You cannot work hard enough to make things happen for your benefit and prosperity if it is outside of His will for you. You cannot choose the wrong paths and expect Him to bless your wrong decisions.

LOOK WITHIN

*"Therefore then, since we are surrounded by so great a cloud of witnesses
[who have borne testimony to the Truth], let us strip off and throw
aside every encumbrance (unnecessary weight) and that sin which so
readily (deftly and cleverly) clings to and entangles us, and let us
run with patient endurance and steady and active persistence
the appointed course of the race that is set before us…"*
Hebrews 12:1 (AMP)

What are you allowing to linger in your life that is keeping you from God's righteousness? Think there is nothing? Look more closely. The encumbrances Paul mentions in Hebrews 12:1 are usually found hiding in the day- to- day things we accept as normal in our world today. Every day we expose our children to pornography on maga-zine racks, in commercials, and in TV shows. We allow cursing in the movies we watch as families and we become addicted to TV programs which are built upon themes that defy the Word of God. We fall victim to the standards of the world in the way we dress, talk, and behave. Now, before you label me a prude or some religious nut, stop and think about it. For your sake, for the sake of your family and future descendants, and for the sake of your destiny, listen for that still small voice of the Holy Spirit. Allow His conviction to come upon you. Take the responsibility you need to take in order to set aside the complacency which has become a part of your daily routine. Trust me, I know the results of not listening, I have lived with them. Don't make excuses for yourself. Don't look for all of the reasons why these things are acceptable. Don't sell yourself or your family short. Remember, you must choose whom you will serve. Choose God and His ways today. Your destiny is waiting.

SECTION I • GETTING TO KNOW YOU

3   Why Are You Here?

*"And do not be conformed to this world, but be transformed by the
renewing of your mind, that you may prove what is that good
and acceptable and perfect will of God."*
Romans 12:2 (NKJV)

*"There are two great days in a person's life – the day we are born
and the day we discover why."*
William Barclay

Do you plod through life sensing you have missed something
along the way? Are you merely surviving while you watch others
around you thrive? When you hear people talk about the will of God,
do you wonder why His will for you appears be that of heartache and
despair? You are not alone. Every day, everywhere, people exist day to
day waiting for the kids to grow up, waiting for retirement, waiting for
their ship to come in, or waiting for someone to fix their problems.
Now, I am not a Bible scholar or a theologian, but based on years
of study, I have discovered some truths about the will of God in His
Word. These truths will help pull you out of the waiting game and
propel you toward your destiny.

Your heavenly Father did not put you here on this great earth to
merely exist or to live a mundane, boring life. Nor did He intend for
you to hectically spend your time trying to please everyone around you

or seeking your own pleasure, fame, and fortune. No, you were created for one purpose and that is to bring glory to your Father in heaven through His will for man generally and for you personally.

Finding God's will for man is as simple as reading His Word. Throughout the pages of Scripture, God clearly defines His general will for man. Once we have accepted Jesus Christ as our Savior, we know from reading that we are to:

1. Follow the Ten Commandments. As Zig Ziglar has stated, *"If God would have wanted us to live in a permissive society He would have given us Ten Suggestions and not Ten Commandments."*

2. Seek righteousness, which is perfect conformity to God's will. In Isaiah 54:14, the prophet writes, *"In righteousness, you will be established."* Would you like to be established in God's will for you? Then seek His righteousness.

3. Be repentant (Romans 2:4). This repentance will help you receive God's will for you.

4. Give thanks to God in ALL circumstances. (1 Thessalonians 5:18) Notice the word all. Good or bad, give thanks.

5. We are to do "good". (1 Peter 2:15) This means to all people as unto the Lord!

6. And we are to love, which is the greatest commandment of all.

This summarizes God's will for man in a nutshell, but in His grace and mercy He goes one step further because He fashioned a perfect will for you individually! How do you discover that treasure? By knowing the gifts He graciously bestowed upon you and by using them to bring Him glory, you will discover the revelation of His will for you. That's why it is so important to know who you are and Whose you are, because when you know that, your passion and purpose will spring forth. When passion is birthed, the warrior inside you arises and no fear can keep you from accomplishing your purpose. Oh, please understand me here. God does have a special will for you. You were not an accident. You were not a second thought. You were designed by the creator of the universe. He birthed you for this moment in time. Whether you are eighteen or eighty-one, He has a plan for you. He has a purpose designed with you in mind!

THE THREE R'S

Society once believed that if a child learned the three R's (reading, wRiting and aRithmetic), he would be equipped for life in the real world. I find the same truths apply for discovering God's perfect will for your life. If you follow the three R's, you will find your purpose. What are the three R's? They are Repentance, Revelation, and Righteousness.

The first step is to repent. It never ceases to amaze me to learn how few Christians actually repent after their initial salvation, and if they do, you will usually find them repenting for the so-called big sins. You know the ones I am talking about—adultery, fornication, theft, murder, and the obliteration of all human decency. But what about the brokenness which comes before breakthrough? It is in that place of conviction that you will find the need to repent if you have denied your gifts, followed your will instead of His, ignored good advice from godly people, or cast judgment upon yourself or others. I want to be clear and assure you that I am in no way recommending you live a life of self-condemnation. Conviction is from the Holy Spirit and is useful for edification. On the other hand, condemnation is from the Devil and is meant to destroy you. When conviction does come, quickly repent so that condemnation has no ground for accusation. As you do this, the veil will be lifted from your eyes and you will be able to see clearly the path before you. There is such freedom in repentance. It is never easy, but when the weight of sin is left at the foot of the cross, the load becomes bearable and the path becomes clear. And in that sweet surrender, God reveals Himself.

We all long to hear the still small voice of the Father. I find that prayer and fasting are essential for accomplishing this. Oh, yes, you read correctly, fasting. But don't take my word. Search His Word yourself, and you will find that prayer and fasting go hand in hand when one is seeking clarity of purpose. The disciples discovered this. Jesus knew it, as did John the Baptist, King David, King Jehoshaphat, Elijah, Esther, Moses, Paul, Nehemiah, and countless others. Fasting opens your ears and closes your mouth! And when I say fasting, I mean really fasting. Fasting by definition is "willingly abstaining from some or all food, drink, or both, for a period of time." In our culture where we are controlled by our stomachs, fasting requires willpower, but it is essential to true spiritual growth. Whenever I fast, I die a little more to me, which enables me to live a little more for Him. So, whether it is a one, two, or three day liquid fast, a twenty-one day Daniel fast, or a combination of both, fasting will draw you closer to God and will your ears to hear His purposes for you. There is no better way to hear His revelation. When you know His plan for you, your faith will overcome the paralysis of fear. Don't let anything hinder your hearing from God because that revelation will lead you to a life of righteousness.

Finally, a life of repentance and revelation will lead you to a life of righteousness. This is not a righteousness of your own lest you boast. But as Paul stated in Philippians 3:9, *"Not having a righteousness of my own that comes from the law, but that which is through faith in Christ—the righteousness that comes from God and is by faith."* Jesus told us to seek His kingdom (found through repentance and revelation) and His righteousness and then *"all these things shall be given to you as well"* (Matthew 6:33). He makes this declaration in a chapter about worry. There is a lot to worry about today, but God wants His people to seek Him and trust Him to work all things out for their good. God tells us in His Word that *"you will seek Me and find Me when you seek Me with all your heart"* (Jeremiah 29:13). Seek Him daily and choose to live out His will for you. If you stay within the three R's, you will live a life of victory as you glorify God in all you do. The best way to glorify Him is to do what He called you to do, so let's find your passion.

PURPOSE WITH PASSION

"When you discover your mission, you will feel its demand.
It will fill you with enthusiasm and a burning desire
to get to work on it."
W. Clement Stone

Have you ever been in a restaurant enjoying a nice meal with a friend when suddenly you hear someone across the room speak a word that causes your pulse to rise? It might be a place you lived, a sport you enjoy, a hobby you love, or a cause you support. Remember that excitement? Suddenly drawn to the stranger seated across the room, you want to jump out of your seat, run over, pull up a chair, and join in the conversation, but instead, you settle for leaning your head in their direction hoping they would talk louder about this shared passion.

What words make you feel that way? What makes your heart leap with excitement at just the mention of its existence? These are your passion words. These are the things that give you more energy than ten cups of coffee, but without the shakes associated with the caffeine. Take a moment right now to list your three passion words. Do not intellectualize this process; let it come from the heart. It will be more effective if you list the first three words that come to you. Do it now.

1. _____

2. _____

3. _____

To give you an example, my passion words are: philanthropy, inspire, and destiny. Is it any wonder I love to give, to inspire people, and to help others accomplish their destiny? Completing this exercise helped me identify my purpose, and it will help you too.

The passion words exercise is a great tool for finding out about others as well. As a leader, it can be used to better understand your team. As a spouse, it can bring about a deeper appreciation between husbands and wives. And it can be used at parties or Bible study groups, which is where it was developed. I must give credit here to my amazing sister-in-law, Jennifer Morris, who came up with the idea. This exercise had such an impact on my life that I borrowed her idea and expanded on it. I have used it in developing a greater appreciation for my friends and associates and in inspiring my listeners when I speak and train.

I realize everyone has different passion words for a reason. We all have unique callings. If you want to live a life of meaning and excitement, live by your passion words. Take a moment now to analyze at your life. Go back to the "Who Am I" exercise and compare your answers. Do these words fit into your daily routine in any way? Do they line up with your identity? Are you living a life that expresses your passion in these areas? If the answer is no, take the time to evaluate all of the good things you are doing. Begin to purposefully focus on your identity and your passion, so that you can discover God's perfect will for you.

Living your passion keeps your mind excited and full of ideas, and it keeps fear at bay. When fear does sneak in, you will not tolerate its distractions in any way. Living life with passion and purpose, while walking in God's perfect will creates an unbreakable line of defense against fear. Remember, you are in a battle for your destiny. As a soldier with something to live and fight for, you now need a battle cry!

WANTED: MIGHTY WARRIORS

"It is courage, courage, courage that raises the blood of life to crimson splendor."
George Bernard Shaw

It is one of those days again. You know the ones. The hands of depression have captured you, squeezing out your last ounce of energy. Your well planned schedule has been flushed down the toilet along with the dreams you should have accomplished by now. Your children appear to have suddenly been taken over by aliens as they fly around the living room, yelling, screaming, and fighting. Your spouse hasn't so much as touched you once yet today. It is just one of those days. You want to wake up and find it was all a bad dream, but no, this is reality, and it happens to the best of us.

Because of days like these you must arm yourself with a battle cry.

This proclamation captures your life purpose, vision, and destiny in one succinct sentence. You will wield this phrase as you stand against the attacks hurled at you from the enemy camp. The release of these words works much like the shout of the Israelites aimed at the city of Jericho. Joshua instructed the people to *"Shout! For the Lord has given you the city!"* (Joshua 6:16). When the shout rang out from the obedient lips of the Israelites, the walls of Jericho came tumbling down. And so it will be when you stand up and tell your adversary fear that you have given control of this land to your God. The deafening ring of your proclamation in the enemy's ears will make him turn tail and run.

So what is this magical phrase, and how do you get one for yourself? Actually, there is nothing magical about it. All you are speaking is truth about who you are and what your purpose is for being here. Are you ready to get a battle cry for yourself? I will give you the beginning of the statement, but you must complete it by working through the previous exercises. If you have finished those, this one should be easy. If you have not finished them, go back now and do them. As you learn about overcoming the paralysis of fear in the coming chapters, you will need all of the ammunition possible, and you will use this powerful phrase quite often. I speak from experience!

Your proclamation begins with: "I am a mighty warrior of the Most High God, put here to..." Now you complete the statement. Mine looks like this. "I am a mighty warrior of the Most High God, put here to help people accomplish their destiny." That is what I do. I coach, write, speak, train, and inspire people to live out their destinies. When I learned the power behind this statement, I suddenly found the freedom to be and do all that God intended. When my purpose became very clear, I then became able to live within the destiny that

God had called me to live, and you will too.

Finish your statement now. Write it out on a piece of paper and memorize it. When the world begins to tell you who you are, stop them in their tracks and tell them who you are. You are a mighty warrior of the Most High God, put here for purposes greater than your own to glorify your Father in Heaven. Become acquainted with the person God called you to be. You may just like who you meet.

THE SEED OF GREATNESS

"I will praise You, for I am fearfully and wonderfully made;
Marvelous are Your works,
And that my soul knows very well."
Psalm 139:14 NKJV

God created you for a purpose. Believe this truth no matter what you have been told by your parents, your spouse, or your best friend. Regardless of how many times you have been lied to, or how insignificant you may think you are, God created you *"for such a time as this"* (Esther 4:14). Everyone has a purpose here. Your purpose can only be lived out by you. No one God brings into this life is insignificant. He knows every hair on your head. He knows your every concern. He knows your every hurt. Nothing is hidden from Him.

I love Charles Swindoll's eloquent description of our purpose for living. What incredible words of wisdom from one of the great leaders of our time:

> The tragedy of all tragedies is that we should live and die having never found that purpose, that special, God-ordained reason for serving our generation. You have, like no other person on this planet, particular contributions that you are to make to

this generation. They may not be as great as your dreams, or they might be far beyond your expectations, but whatever they are, you are to find them and carry them out.

Charles Swindoll, David: A Man of Passion and Destiny

You were fearfully and wonderfully made in the image of the most High God. Before the beginning of time, He implanted in each person without exception a seed of greatness. And if there are no exceptions this means you too have a seed planted within you. He intends for you to find that seed. He does not want you to go through this life and not live out the purpose that He called you here to accomplish. I do not know your purpose, but I am confident God does. He desires that you find it, nurture it, sustain it, and live fully within your destiny!

Frequently, garbage comes along and covers up the un-sprouted seed within you. You may be wondering what I mean by garbage. The garbage is your fears, the lies others have spoken over you, the preconceived ideas you carry around, and the limits you place on yourself. It is unresolved anger, frustration, and unrealistic expectations you place on yourself or others. You hold yourself hostage in a box because of all of these self-imposed limitations. Garbage will always clutter up your life. It will always keep you bound and distracted, and it will always keep your seed hidden and malnourished.

I was once a garbage collector, maybe you have been one too. But I learned how to get rid of the rubbish, so that the gifts within me could take root. The clear realities of who I am and Whose I am enabled me to clean out major garbage. How did I do that? Think about the times when you have decided to reorganize the garage or the basement. The task seemed so overwhelming. You piled garbage there for years because you could not figure out what to do with it. Things you were afraid to let go of because they just might be valuable, reminders of your past, and trash you had no time to deal with remained hidden in the dark. Your garage collected dust and invited pestilence into your home. You wondered if you could ever complete the job. You would much rather flee and do something fun, but you could not neglect your responsibility anymore. So you rolled up your sleeves and got to work. When you finished the job, you looked around with great satisfaction. That once dirty, cluttered, dark hole became a usable, functional space. If you are careful, you will never allow it to get out of hand again, but if you fall back into your old ways, you will be faced with the same old problem.

The same is true with your inner self. You need to rid yourself of the garbage which has been covering your seed. Have you ever seen anything green and beautiful growing in a garbage pit? No, because garbage cannot feed the seed. I am not going to kid you here. Getting rid of your garbage will not be any more fun than cleaning out your garage. It will be hard, you will need to deal with some painful experiences, and you may want to quit and stuff it all back inside. But I beg you to stick with it. Get an accountability partner (preferably one who has already been through it), hold tight to your Word and take a stand for your destiny. I believe in you and better yet, God believes in you. That is why He entrusted to you this special gift meant only for you.

It amuses me how we go through life holding on so tightly to our garbage—so unwilling to let go as if it were some sort of priceless treasure as we scream out, "Don't take my garbage! It is my identity. It is who I am!" And yet we run, hide, whine, and complain about (not to be vulgar or offensive) our *crap*. And yes, I said crap! I wish there were some other way to say it, but I use this word for a reason. Crap is your history—the things that just happen to you. It is the car accident, the cancer, the abuse, the death of a loved one, the divorce, the neglect, the heartache, the disappointments, the failures, the mistakes, the bankruptcy, the foreclosure, the failed business, the lost retirement, the disease. These things all stink and are messy. As much as we want to avoid them, as much as we resent them for happening to us, we must stop and ponder the question of where we would be without them. Crap is everything that has made you who you are today. Everything you have gone through, everything, God intended for your greater good. If He allowed it, it is to be used in your growth. Most of us would have a pretty boring story if we hadn't been through the things we have been though. Dave Ramsey, Christian author and radio host on finance, might not have a ministry at all had he not been through more than one bankruptcy. I cannot imagine what I would ever speak or write about if I had not experienced the times of testing and trial which have impacted my life in profound ways. Character is not birthed in times of peace but in times of adversity. Fine wine can only be made by the crushing of perfectly good grapes. Instead of seeing our crap for what it is—a character developer—we complain about it. We take the crap and flush it while we cling to our garbage. What we don't realize is that the seed within us cannot grow in the garbage, but crap is fertilizer! If you have garbage clean out day, get rid of destructive fears and lies and then till the crap around your seed; God will water it with His Word. He will send people into your life to feed it, and He will even send the Holy Spirit—your Miracle Grow—which will nourish your seed and replace what the locusts have eaten. And before you know it, your magnificent, one-of-a-kind seed will be sprouting.

Something spectacular happens when we find our seed and begin to realize our true value in Christ. We begin to see that this God-given seed was not planted in us so that we could glorify ourselves but so we could glorify our Father in heaven.

Rick Warren's book, *The Purpose Driven Life*, has impacted millions of lives. His thoughts in the first chapter really capture the truth of what your life purpose is all about. He wrote, "The purpose of your life is far greater than your own personal fulfillment, your peace of mind, or even your happiness. It's far greater than your family, your career, or even your wildest dreams and ambitions. If you want to know why you were placed on this planet, you must begin with God. You were born by His purpose and for His purpose."

When you look at your life through God's lens, you will then discover your seed of greatness which has evaded you far too long. Don't join the throngs who believe this seed of greatness is reserved for an elite group. Maybe you can relate to a woman I met at a seminar I gave on overcoming the paralysis of fear. I will call her Ida.

From outward appearances, Ida appeared to be a happy, even jovial woman full of joy, but as God tells Samuel in 1 Samuel 16:7, "*The Lord does not look at the things man looks at. Man looks at the outward appearance, but the Lord looks at the heart.*" We so quickly judge the outward appearance of man, but we need to look deeper. During the seminar, God revealed this woman's heart.

My compassion for Ida increased as I taught that day. I continued to pray that something I said would lift the yoke from her, but nothing did. After I ended the seminar, everyone left, but she remained. She needed answers. She was once fearless and now she lived in continual fear and torment. What was she to do?

We talked, we prayed, and the outpouring of God's love for her caused Ida to break. Her story is not a lot different from countless others who have succumbed to the lie that destinies are only available for a select few. Her eyes focused solely on herself and her past identity, and she became blinded to God's plans for her. If you are looking back, you will not be able to see where you are going. Looking back and dwelling on your failures and even your successes can bring regret. You will either regret what you did or regret what you didn't do. You may even regret that you are no longer the person you once were. Either way, you will be unproductive and unable to hear from God, find your seed, and live out your purpose.

"But Lot's wife looked back, and she became a pillar of salt."
Genesis 19:26

Lot's wife made the fatal mistake of looking back. Genesis 19 reveals the danger of staying in our past when God is moving us toward a better prospect. Lot and his family were escaping judgment. The alternative for them would have been certain death. The Lord had shown them favor, but they were told not to linger and not to look back as they fled. What came over Lot's wife as the family moved into a more promising future? What made her not only look back, but linger long enough to be caught up in the fire and brimstone that fell on Sodom and Gomorrah and as a result turn to a pillar of salt? The place she left was evil. Had she become accustomed to it? Did she have other children there who had refused to escape with them, and instead of being thankful for the two she had with her, was she longing for the ones who had chosen evil over God? We will never know since there is nothing else written about Lot's wife. But the lesson we learn from her is invaluable. Your past is just that—it is your past. You cannot repeat it, you cannot relive it, you cannot redo it, and you cannot live in its glory or change its outcome. Lot's wife was holding onto her garbage, so was Ida. She needed to drop her bags of useless trash, protect her seed, and live out her destiny, but she didn't. Will you?

CONCLUSION

"The Lord will fulfill His purpose for me, Your love, O Lord,
endures forever- do not abandon the works of Your hands."
Psalm 138:8

We have just spent the first several chapters revealing the truth about who you are, Whose you are, and what your purpose is in being here, because great victory comes from warriors who know why they are fighting, what they are fighting, and who they are fighting for. I hope that by now, you believe that you were put here for a purpose. I hope you have discovered your incredible value to God and to the world around you. And I pray that by now you have decided that your destiny is worth fighting for, because it is. So let me remind you as move forward that you are a mighty warrior of the Most High God put here for purposes only you can accomplish.

This essential knowledge will not be enough. To confidently defeat fear in battle, you will need to slip quietly into the enemy camp and retrieve information which will guarantee your success. A large part of your war strategy derives from knowing your enemy. According to military experts about 90 percent of the key to a triumphant battle relies on espionage, so let's go get it.

"Life is not just a few years to spend in self-indulgence and career
advancement. It is a privilege, a responsibility, a stewardship
to be lived according to a much higher calling."
Elizabeth Dole

DEFEATING FEAR

SECTION 2

KNOW YOUR ENEMY

"But my righteous one will live by faith, and if he shrinks back,
I will not be pleased with him."
Hebrews 10:38

"Fear defeats more people than any other one thing in the world."
Ralph Waldo Emerson

DEFEATING FEAR

SECTION 2 • KNOW YOUR ENEMY

4   Where Fear and Faith Collide

*"There is no fear in love. But perfect love drives out fear,
because fear has to do with punishment."*
1 John 4:18

*"It has been said that our anxiety does not empty tomorrow
of its sorrow, but only empties today of its strength."*
Charles Haddon Spurgeon

Some things will just never go together like oil and water, good
and evil, black socks and sandals. Some things were destined to be
separated. Fear and faith also cannot co-exist. It is impossible. Just as
far as light is from darkness, so far is faith from fear. Faith will cast out
fear, but just as quickly, fear will cast out faith.

The experts resort to psycho-analyzing fear. But this approach is
like dealing with the symptoms of a disease instead of curing the disease itself. I believe this faulty thinking has led many in our world today to rely on prescription drugs to get out of bed in the morning. You
cannot deal logically with a foe that is anything but logical. Fear does
not play fair. It does not follow the rules of the game. It lies, cheats,
seduces, steals, traps, and snares. Fear will speak to you through your
spouse, your best friend, your boss, the evening news, your favorite
program, and even your own family. It shows no partiality, for all have

fallen victim to it. God's greats, the heroes of the faith, each experienced fear at one time or another. What set them apart, and what will set you apart too, is that their faith was greater than their fear.

UNDERSTANDING YOUR FEAR

"Courage is the resistance of fear, the mastery of fear,
not the absence of fear."
Mark Twain

Between 1875 and 1883, Black Bart robbed twenty-nine Wells Fargo stage coaches which were carrying people full of dreams to a better life out West. His weapon was his reputation, and it was quite powerful. Many people gave up their dream to go West because of the fear they had of this fearless man.

Black Bart wore a mask. No artist ever sketched him; no victim caught a glimpse of his face. He was as mysterious as he seemed fearless. And yet, in all the years that he paralyzed people with fear, he never fired a shot and no one was injured at his hands. Still, fear reigned at the mention of his name.

When the authorities finally caught up with Black Bart they discovered some pretty interesting facts. First of all, his name was Charles E. Boles, a mild mannered druggist from Decatur, Illinois. Second, when this fearless man was unmasked, they found out that Mr. Boles was actually full of fear. For one, he was afraid of horses. As a matter of fact, he would ride a buggy as far as he could before he would switch to horseback for the last leg of the trip to his next robbery. The authorities also discovered that there was a reason Black Bart never fired a shot in his thirteen year reign of terror. He never loaded his gun!

A man full of fear gained a reputation of being fearless because of his lies and his victims' imagination. This story says a lot about our fears. Many of the fears that taunt us, kick us around, and leave us intimidated really do not have any substance at all. They are merely masked lies, and all we need to do is expose them for what they are.

To reach your Promised Land you will need to unmask some Black Barts in your life. Until you do, you will continue to live and walk in fear, and like many of the people who were too afraid to go west, you too will remain on the sidelines of life, never reaching your destiny.

FINDING YOUR WAY THROUGH THE FOG

The oppressiveness of fog reminds me of the oppressiveness of fear. When you are in fear you cannot see beyond your thoughts and emotions. You lose the ability to cast your eyes on the horizon where all hope lies. When you find yourself engulfed in the fog of fear you may not be able to see your Promised Land. But the knowledge you have acquired tells you it is there. You know it, because you have been there before. You have lost a job and found a better one. You have lost a loved one and learned to breathe again. You have elected presidents you feared would bring destruction only to find you made it through to a new election. You have run the marathon, delivered the baby, asked for the raise, made the presentation, asked the person out, survived the first date, climbed the mountain, passed the test, confronted your spouse, and most importantly, you survived. In this life there is one thing you do know. The sun will rise again. The fog will lift, the storm will pass, and the things you fear today will seem frivolous tomorrow. The key is not allowing fear to stifle you in the process.

Fog is a quirky thing. It seems to settle in a place, get comfortable, and stick around for a while. Fog, like fear, blinds you to the truth. It plays with your mind and causes you to see things as they really are... not! Have you ever tried to drive in a thick fog? Everything looks different. The roads you have driven for years now appear unknown. You miss the turn at the stop sign. You cannot remember where the bend in the road is up ahead or even forget there is one. Your knowledge of this road vanishes as you allow the fog to control you rather than trusting the wisdom within you. When you allow fear to permeate your mind, you invite the dense fog of deception into your thoughts and emotions. Suddenly, you find you cannot see the horizon. You are blinded to all you knew to be true. The difference between fear and fog, though, is that unlike fog, you have the ability to choose to lift fear from your life. You are not controlled by weather patterns in your mind. You can take captive the thoughts that bring fear and replace them with thoughts that bring life.

LOOKING WITHIN

Would you like to reveal, expose, and take dominion over the endless list of fears which have been holding you back? I am certain that if you take the time to do this exercise you will find great freedom in it. It is not hard, but it will require complete honesty. There is no need to share it with anyone unless you choose to, but you need to take the time to do it. By investing the time, you will find the freedom you need to step out of fear and into faith.

This exercise began when a friend told me that I could not effectively minster to others until I had taken dominion over the fears I had been living with. The challenge shocked me because I thought

I had come such a long way. I pondered this for a while until I felt compelled to act. I sat down with a legal pad and began listing every fear I've ever had. Talk about enlightenment. First, the length of the list astounded me, and second, the number of things I still feared horrified me. I discovered through this process how closely associated many of my fears were.

I put the finished list aside, not knowing what to do next. I spoke with another friend that day and shared what I had done. A little while later I received a text from her telling me to write the opposite of each fear. I inquired why. She replied that she had no idea, but I would know when the time was right. I went right back to my list and wrote down the opposites of all of my fears. This was moving. There was power in it. Suddenly, I felt compelled to write a faith statement using my list. With that act came freedom. I felt liberated. I felt empowered. And I had a new invaluable sense of understanding about myself.

Today is the day to unmask your Black Barts. This exercise will prepare you for the incredible journey on which you are embarking. I am so excited for you because this unveiling will prepare you to leave the wilderness and to enter the Promised Land.

When you are ready (and please do not let fear talk you out of this), get out a piece of paper and a pen and go through the following steps. I have included examples with each one so that there will be no doubts in your mind as to what you are to do. Have fun, be honest with yourself, and prepare for a prison break!

Step 1 - Begin by making a list of all of the fears you have encountered in your lifetime. Take the time to address all of them no matter how insignificant they seem. Trust me, if you have feared it before, you will fear it again if you do not replace it with faith.

Step 2 - Next to each fear list its opposite. For example, if you fear death the opposite would be life. If you fear criticism, the opposite would be praise. Continue doing this until you have an opposite listed for all your fears.

Step 3 - Once you have finished the first two steps develop a faith statement for yourself. You will do this by taking your list of opposites and making declarations about them. I recommend you use a lot of Scripture in your statement, since using Scripture will remind you every time you read it that God's Word is true, and there is power in reading it out loud. Hebrews 4:12 states it so well, *"For the word of God is living and active. Sharper than any double-edged sword, it penetrates even to dividing soul and spirit, joints and marrow; it judges the thoughts and attitudes of the heart."* My long list made my faith statement long also, so I will not include the whole thing here. But just so you can get the idea I will share an abbreviated sample with you.

FEAR	OPPOSITE	STATEMENT
Heights	Level Ground	I walk on level ground. I fear God and God
Loss	Gain	alone. What can man do to me? No weapon
Man	God	formed against me can prosper, therefore
Failure	Success	I live in gain with great success.

Step 4 – Read your statement aloud every morning and every night for thirty days. Commit it to memory so that when the lie of fear tries to rear its ugly head you are ready. You may initially need to repeat it several times a day to yourself. But as the words sink into the recesses of your mind, your strength will rise up and prepare you to take on your giants.

......

Knowledge is power. You need power for the battle, but you will not defeat fear with knowledge alone. The information you will discover about yourself and your enemy in this exercise will gird you up and prepare you for battle, but without the shield of faith, any victory will be short lived. As we move ahead, you will learn how to go beyond knowledge. But, let's not get ahead of ourselves here. In order to get beyond knowledge, you must first get knowledge.

GET KNOWLEDGE

"Every prudent man acts out of knowledge, but a fool exposes his folly."
Proverbs 13:16

When studying Proverbs 4, I was taken aback by all of the action steps that were listed in those lines regarding wisdom. Listen, pay attention, gain, lay hold of, keep, get, do not forget, do not forsake, love, watch over, esteem, embrace, listen, accept, walk, run, hold, etc. You get the picture. The verb that really caught my attention though, was the word get. In verse 5, Solomon tells us to *"get wisdom, get understanding."* In other words, we are not just to pray for wisdom and understanding, we are to go out there and get it. We are to grasp it, take hold of it, and own it.

The same is true with knowledge. You cannot suddenly become knowledgeable. You must get knowledge. You may wish you could just hold the Bible to your head and acquire the knowledge from it by osmosis, but that will not happen. It requires action to get something. To get knowledge from the Word of God, you will need to open the book and read it, study it, and assimilate it. The same is true with fear. To overcome the paralysis of fear you must understand fear. To understand fear you must acquire knowledge about fear. A great general will never send troops into battle without an understanding of the adversary. He will get understanding and knowledge about the strengths, weaknesses, and strategies of the enemy, so he will best know where, when, and how to attack.

As you prepare to take on the giant of fear, you will need to seek out that knowledge too. You are preparing for battle, so you too should get an understanding of the opposing forces. Just as the fear of God is the beginning of all wisdom, the knowledge of fear is the beginning of your victory over this mortal enemy.

When I felt the call on my life to speak, preach, and share truths of God through the written word, something incredible happened to me. After years of dutifully reading God's Word, I suddenly felt compelled to know God on a deeper level. When someone is important to you, you will ask deeper questions and prod into their lives as you dig up special treasures which make them unique. And that is what God wants of His children. He wants us to get knowledge, get understanding, and get wisdom of who He is. As I dug into His Word, I could not believe the vast treasures I found. Words I had read for years seemed new, like something I had never read before. And as I searched, dug, and devoured the Word of God, I acquired knowledge. That knowledge led me to a deeper faith which introduced me to love like I have never known, and in that love, there was an absence of fear.

WORDS OF POWER

"There is no fear in love. But perfect love drives out fear,
because fear has to do with punishment."
1 John 4:18

The entire Bible is filled with one example after another of God's people, anointed and appointed by Him, who at some point were overcome with fear. Some, like King Jehoshaphat, knew they needed to turn quickly to God for help; some, like King Saul, lost their anointing all together because they allowed fear to control them. Even the great Paul had moments of fear. But success comes when your faith is greater than your fear. If you think you can keep your faith strong enough to overcome the constant onslaught of fear in your life without the knowledge of God and His Word, you are fooling yourself. In your own strength, you cannot withstand the arrows meant for your defeat. But when you walk in His strength, you will walk in victory. You will be shod to enter into battle. You will be girded up with weapons which may not make sense to man. And although fear may attack you from all directions, your faith in God and your knowledge of His truth will be your defense.

When the Devil tempted Jesus in the wilderness, what weapon did He use? He used the very Word of God. Matthew 4 recounts the story for us and teaches us some great lessons. After the first temptation, Jesus said to the Devil in verse 4 *"...Man does not live on bread alone, but on every word that comes from the mouth of God."* If Jesus lived by and depended on the Word of God, why should we think we don't need to?

When the Devil came to Him a second time, Jesus was tempted to test God. Have you ever been tempted to do that? I think we all have.

We think "Oh God, if you are really there, prove it to me by…". This is what the Devil was saying to Jesus. *"Throw yourself down so that the angels will lift you up."* Jesus could have done this, but instead He said in verse 7 *"…Do not put the Lord your God to the test."* When we truly trust someone, we will never test their love for us. That is the lesson here. We need to trust God so much and to love Him so deeply that even if He never did another thing for us, we would love Him still. He owes us nothing. The fact that we are living and breathing is more than we should expect from this God we have defiled, turned against, falsified, cheated and forsaken. Thank God for His endless mercy and amazing grace!

Finally, the Devil gave it one more shot, and here we learn two great lessons, one of them from the Devil himself. Have you ever noticed how he does not just try to derail us one time and then give up? If we could have the tenacity of the Devil, but the power and righteousness of God, we would be a force to be reckoned with! This time, the Devil decided he would get Jesus where he knew most men were weak. He offered Him the world. Power and prestige would be His for the taking. There was only one small catch. Jesus needed to bow down and worship him. The final blow came when Jesus rebuked him in verse 10 *"…Away from me, Satan! For it is written: 'Worship the Lord your God and serve him only.'"* Oh the power of the words Jesus spoke. *"Away from me, Satan!"* That is the final lesson here. If you remember no other Scripture, if under attack and nothing else comes to your mind, this one line will be a fiery dart into the enemy camp. It will strike with precision and destroy its target. *"Away from me, Satan!"* will hurl forth from your sling shot with the accuracy of David's meager stone as it penetrates the skull of your Goliath.

As you step over from fear to faith you will be transformed from the natural world to the supernatural realm. This is where battles are fought, victories are gained, and destinies are claimed. So let's step over with the turning of this page, from bondage to freedom, and from fear to faith.

SECTION 2 · KNOW YOUR ENEMY

5   Unshakable Faith

"Now faith is the assurance of things hoped for,
the conviction of things not seen."
Hebrews 11:1

"A person of courage is also full of faith."
Marcus Tullius Cicero

In 1952, Florence Chadwick set out to swim the twenty-six miles between Catalina Island and the California coastline. During her attempt, a thick, oppressive fog set in, inhibiting her from seeing her destination. After fighting for the new world record for sixteen hours, Florence's doubts got the best of her and she stopped swimming one half mile from shore. She later said, "All I could see was the fog, I think if I could have seen the shore, I would have made it."

Many victories are lost just inches from the finish line. Many people fight for their lives, but when the results do not come fast enough, fear begins to take over. This mocking liar tells them they will be a laughing stock because they have wasted their time, effort, money, and energy on such a harebrained idea. And then just a half a mile from the shoreline, they stop simply because they cannot see the coast.

Maybe this has been your story. Perhaps you have stopped just inches from the finish line because you chose to listen to the opinions of everyone around you - those who were too fearful to even enter the race. Maybe your faith has not been as strong as your fear and you have listened to the louder voice. Maybe you just haven't known how to build up your faith, so that you could walk victoriously through the battlefield to your destiny. Maybe you have been overwhelmed by failure because you dared at one time to believe the impossible, but later gave up, and now you have lost all hope for your future.

Is your dream impossible? Are you unable to see beyond the next few steps? Are you wondering if you will beat this illness, salvage your retirement, save your house, or accomplish the things God has laid on your heart to do? Did you answer yes? Great, because your God is a God who does the impossible! Jesus did great things and took on the impossible cases. He healed hemorrhaging, not mild headaches. He calls His people to be people of faith, and even tells us *"without faith it is impossible to please God"* (Hebrews 11:6).

How do you know if you are walking in faith? It will be obvious. It is a lack of faith when you think it all depends on you. In faith, you will have no way out other than with God alone. In faith, your plans will be His plans, and the only fall back plan you will have will be when you fall back behind Him and allow Him to be God. In faith you will know and believe that nothing is impossible with God if you are living out His will for your life. In faith, you will not be saying, "Can I?" but rather "God can." When you are walking in faith, you will know there is no chance of success at all if it is up to you alone. Fear will dominate your thought life and will rob you of sleep, peace, and all enthusiasm, but faith will restore you and will mount you up with wings as eagle so that you will run and not grow weary; you will walk and not grow faint (paraphrased from Isaiah 40:31).

Did you know it takes the same amount of energy to live in fear as it does to live in faith? One, however, brings with it misery and failure, while the other brings with it success and happiness. There are several common denominators between the two though. Both fear and faith demand that you believe something is going to happen in your life which you cannot see. Both dominate your thought life and control your emotions. Both are highly contagious. And both are a choice only you can make for yourself. One will bring with it misery and destruction while cursing your future generations. The other will bring with it a future of hope with blessings and a heritage that will be handed down to your children as well as your children's children. Why not choose faith?

When you walk in faith, the world may tell you that you can't, but faith will scream, "You can!" When you fall, faith will give you strength to get back up again. When you think you can't go on, faith will tell you to give it one more try. When others say you never will, faith will prove them wrong time and time again.

Don't let fear talk you out of your God-given destiny. Fear will distort your perspective. Your negative thoughts will only turn to negative manifestations unless you choose to let your mind run wild with faith. Remember, it takes just as much energy to think in faith as it does to think in fear, but when you think in faith, you will be a happier person with whom others will enjoy associating. When you walk in faith, you will not be able to help yourself speak life and not death into the lives of your children and grandchildren, your spouse and your coworkers, your friends and your family members. As believers, we are called to exhort and encourage one another. How can you do that effectively if you are meditating on fear? What you think, you will speak. To speak life and hope, your mind and heart must be full of both.

LORD, INCREASE MY FAITH

You may be tempted right now to beat yourself up over your lack of faith, but before you go there, read on…

> *"And the apostles said to the Lord, 'Increase our faith!'"*
> *Luke 17:5*

Why did the apostles need Jesus to increase their faith? These men of God had been hand selected by the Lord Himself to disciple under Him. They had witnessed the miracle working power of Jesus Christ for three solid years. They watched Him calm the storms, walk on water, raise Lazarus from the dead , cure diseases, destroy demons, and turn water into wine; yet we find them in both Matthew 17 and Luke 17 asking, no, actually demanding that Jesus increase their faith. If the disciples who worked side by side with Jesus on a daily basis for three years found themselves needing their faith strengthened, why are we so ashamed when we need to be restored? And better yet, why are we so judgmental when other believers seem to be lacking in their faith?

DRESS ACCORDINGLY

> *"…take up the shield of faith, with which you can extinguish all the*
> *flaming arrows of the evil one."*
> *Ephesians 6:16*

Ephesians 6:10-20 is a powerful section of Scripture to study when it comes to overcoming the paralysis of fear. Let's take a closer look at it.

> *Finally, be strong in the Lord and in His mighty power. Put on the full armor of God so that you can take your stand against the Devil's schemes. For our struggle is not against flesh and blood, but against the rulers, against the authorities, against the powers of this dark world and against the spiritual forces of evil in the heavenly realms. Therefore put on the full armor of God, so that when the day of evil comes, you may be able to stand your ground, and after you have done everything, to stand.*
> *Ephesians 6:10-13*

Let's stop here for a moment and take note of several key words in this passage. First, Paul instructs us to be strong in the Lord and in the power of His might. Notice that he said nothing about your might or power. In your own power you are nothing and can do nothing, but in His power you can do all things He destines you to do. You may have had success in the world, and you may be at the top in your field today, but if you hold that position in your own power, there will be someone waiting in the wings to overpower you. But if God places you in leadership, you will hold that position as long as He needs you there.

> *"And David knew that the Lord had established him as king over Israel and that his Kingdom had been highly exalted for the sake of his people Israel."*
> *1 Chronicles 14:2*

The second thing Paul tells us is that there is something we need to do for ourselves and that is to put on the full armor of God. Notice that he does not say to do it occasionally or whenever we feel like the enemy may attack. We need to do this task daily. It was as if Paul knew that our complacency would make us vulnerable to the enemy lurking about who takes no holiday, has no concern for us, and wishes nothing but our destruction. Should you go about blaming all of your misfortune on him? Certainly not. Many of the challenges we face in this life are actually a form of corrective discipline from our loving Father. Hebrews 12:7 tells us that we should endure hardship as discipline. That discipline creates a harvest of righteousness. There are also many things we go through simply because we chose to do things our way. Rebellion, lack of wisdom, and stubbornness will often bring with them nothing but misery. You are responsible for your behavior. Blaming the Devil for everything bad in your life should not be the way of the believer, but acknowledging his existence and knowing that his intention is to derail your destiny, should cause you to suit up each morning and prepare for battle. Get past the blame game and put on your armor.

Why bother putting on the full armor of God? Paul goes on to explain, "...so you can take your stand against the devil's schemes" (Ephesians 6:11). And what is one of the Devil's greatest schemes? You guessed it, FEAR. This becomes all the more obvious as you read on through verse 12. Paul explains that you are not fighting against people, although there sure are times when it will feel like you are. No, instead he writes that you are fighting "against the rulers, against the authorities, against the powers of this dark world and against the spiritual forces of evil in the heavenly realms" (v.12). This exhortation of Paul reminds me of the best marriage advice my husband and I ever received. We were told to remember when we were fighting that it was not me against him or him against me, but rather us against the problem. The same is true here. You need to learn to separate the people from the principalities as you blaze the trail toward your destiny, because the enemy will use whatever tools are at his disposal to shake you. Close relationships gone bad will have a more devastating effect than any disaster, calamity, or failure you may face.

After Paul informs us of the work in the spirit realm, he goes on to remind us again to put on our armor. He is emphatic here, but why? *"So that WHEN the day of evil comes, you may be able to stand your ground…"* (Ephesians 6:13, emphasis mine). This is obviously not up for debate with Paul. He does not say if, just in case, or should it so happen, but WHEN. Are you surprised when bad things happen to you for no apparent reason? Don't be. Have you had your fair share of heartache, sorrow, and pain? Most have. First, make sure you have taken responsibility for the consequences of any sin you may have committed. Repent and let it go. This will restore fellowship with the Father. Much like when parents have to discipline their children, the goal is always restoration of relationship. Sin divides and repentance unifies. Please understand that I am not in any way saying that all pain and heartache are caused by your sin. Unfortunately, as the saying goes, "Hurt people, hurt people." When that hurt comes, it is important not to allow it to lead you into sin. Make sure you are not carrying around any resentment or bitterness against those who have wrongfully treated you. Keep your heart clean before the Father. However, when you do sin, that is your choice and you need to take responsibility for it. After you have freed yourself from the ball and chain of unrepentence, you will easily be able to slip into the armor of God and boldly declare war on fear. The enemy has had victory over you long enough!

"Stand firm then, with the belt of truth buckled around your waist, with the breastplate of righteousness in place, and with your feet fitted with the readiness that comes from the gospel of peace. In addition to all this, take up the shield of faith, with which you can extinguish all the

flaming arrows of the evil one. Take the helmet of salvation
and the sword of the Spirit, which is the word of God."
Ephesians 6:12-17

THE WARDROBE OF A WARRIOR

You know now that you need to put on your armor and you know why, but have you ever taken the time to understand the pieces of armor Paul instructs you to wear? If you find yourself continually caught in the grip of fear, I can guarantee, you are missing a piece or two of your armor. Reread the passage above and take note of the fact that Paul does not list any optional pieces. He does not merely recommend using the armor. He demands it. He is almost like a commanding officer preparing to send his troops off to battle. "Ten – hut!" Slowly he approaches, glaring at you as he investigates your armor. "Soldier, why is your belt of truth so tattered and loose? There are smudges all over your breastplate. And look at your feet! Where are your shoes? You should be shod with the gospel of peace, yet all I see are muddy feet! Your shield is tarnished. Your helmet is toppled, and where is your sword? Do you really think you can make it through this battle without your sword—the very Word of God?"

While Paul's demanding voice is still ringing through your head, I ask you to think about that question again. Do you really think you can make it through the battle for your destiny without the Word of God and His protective armor? Do you think you can stay married, raise your kids, honor your parents, build a business, lead a community, run a country, or survive any one of life's many challenges without it? Sadly, many think they can, and you see them every day bearing mental and emotional scars from neglecting to wear the full armor of God.

THE BELT OF TRUTH

Each piece of God's armor is not only indispensable, but inde-scribably powerful. Take for example, the belt of truth. Walking in truth in all circumstances will prevent the need to cover up lies and distortions, lessen the stress in your life dramatically, and allow you to walk boldly in your calling. And when you are living in truth, you will also be equipped to discern the truth from a lie. Truth is powerful, and when you wear the belt of truth, it will support the rest of your armor! Do you see what I mean by indispensable? And that's just one piece.

THE BREASTPLATE OF RIGHTEOUSNESS

Because Jesus is our righteousness and it is His righteousness which guards and protects our hearts, the breastplate of righteousness is one all Christians should wear during wartime and peace. But where do you find this fashion necessity? The answer can be found through-out the Word, but Paul says it so well in Romans 3:22 when he writes, *"This righteousness from God comes through faith in Jesus Christ to all who believe."* You cannot create this piece of armor by good works or right thinking; it can only come from one place. Your righteousness will be found in Christ alone. By accepting this priceless gift and then wearing it, you will go forward with confidence knowing you are protected by the righteousness not of yourself but of Christ Jesus. What an awesome gift of grace for those who believe.

THE GOSPEL OF PEACE

I think it is safe to say that most of us prefer good news as opposed to bad. The prophet Isaiah in chapter 52:7 penned, *"How beautiful on the mountains are the feet of those who bring good news, who proclaim peace, who bring glad tidings..."* When your feet are shod in the gospel of peace, you will be the one delivering the good news and glad tidings causing others to be drawn to you and the goodness of God in you. Walking in peace will help you to live joyfully as you actively live out God's purposes for you. The Devil does not want you living in peace on the mountaintop of faith. He would prefer to keep you in the valley of fear looking at yourself and questioning whether you can ever know peace. He will tell you that in order to live at peace with God, you need to be perfect, blameless and flawless, but if you are wearing the gospel of peace, then that peace and the truth it carries with it will prevail when deception hits.

THE SHIELD OF FAITH

The shield Paul tells us about in Ephesians 6 is a great tool to use for deflecting the incoming assaults of the enemy, but it may surprise you to find that the shield he is using as an example is very different from the shields we think of today. Instead of being a little round shield not much bigger than a trash can lid, the Roman shield was a curved rectangle which covered most of the body from the shoulders to the middle of the thigh. When in battle, soldiers could interlock their shields and march together against the enemy, and that is what happens today as we link shields with fellow believers. Faith on your own is powerful, but faith multiplied by aligning with other like-minded believers makes you a force to be reckoned with! Yes, faith moves mountains, tears down strongholds, and destroys the demons of darkness, so be sure not to be caught with your shield down!

THE SWORD OF THE SPIRIT

The sword of the Spirit is the living Word of God. Paul described it best in Hebrews 4:12 when he wrote, *"For the word of God is living and active and sharper than any two-edged sword, and piercing as far as the division of soul and spirit, of both joints and marrow, and able to judge the thoughts and intentions of the heart."* This valuable piece of armor is meant to be used close up. It is for those times when fear is in your face! There is nothing more powerful. Note that Jesus carried no weapons with Him during His time upon this Earth. His weapon against the Devil in Matthew 4 was the Word of God. It cut the Devil and pierced him to his evil core, laying bare his intentions to sabotage our Savior. The sword of the Spirit brought Jesus great victory as you can see in Matthew 4:11, *"Then the Devil left him, and the angels came and attended him."* Do you want to thwart the plans of the Devil and be ministered to by heavenly hosts? Then wield your Sword!

THE HELMET OF SALVATION

And last, but not at all least, is the irreplaceable helmet of salvation which will serve to protect your most vulnerable asset, your mind. The fears which have kept you from your destiny are probably not physical happenings around you. No, instead, they are most likely the thoughts within you. In his book, *Rumors of War*, Phillip Caputo shared a great insight into the way fear works on the mind when he said, "A man needs many things in war, but a strong imagination is not one of them." Your imagination will get you into more trouble, will waste your energy, and will singlehandedly keep you from your purpose more than any other weapon formed against you.

How many times have you feared a divorce, your children dying, your spouse dying, losing your home, being abused, losing your job, being crippled, or being left alone? How many times have you feared failing, being laughed at and mocked, being in an accident, dying, being humiliated, or being shamed by the actions of your kids? It is because of our active imaginations that God took the time to exhort us in His Word when the Apostle Paul wrote, *"Finally brothers, whatever is true, whatever is noble, whatever is right, whatever is pure, whatever is lovely, whatever is admirable—if anything is excellent or praiseworthy—think about such things"* (Philippians 4:8). The brain is powerful. Before you speak, you think, and sometimes in that thinking, you will dwell too long on things which will bring you destruction. The helmet of salvation will keep your thoughts toward God and full of faith.

Which pieces of armor have you been neglecting? Are you walking in peace and living out the Word of God as you go about your day-to-day routine? Are you known for being an honest person? Does your yes mean yes and your no mean no? Are you characterized as a person who can be depended on when you have given your word? Do you seek God on a daily basis so that you will grow in His righteousness? Is your heart right before God? Do you monitor what you watch on TV, what you read, and where you allow your mind to roam? Do you walk in faith, talk in faith, and believe in faith that God is all He says He is and will do all He says He will do? Have you fully submitted all into the hands of your Savior, or are you still trying to control the reigns of your future? Do you wield the sword of the Spirit which is the Word of God in all areas of your life even outside of the church walls? Do you seek it for the solution to your problems and the answers to your questions? Is it the final authority in your life? Do you live and die by this sword?

Just as you have a choice between fear and faith in your life, you also have a choice as to whether you will suit up each morning that God gives you breath. If you want victory in your life, if you want to live a life of faith, if you want to squash the power of fear over your future from this moment on, you will choose the armor of God—every piece of it, every day.

The attacks from the enemy camp will come, but faith accompanied by the full armor of God, will extinguish them all. That is not my opinion. It is God's Word. Can His Word be wrong? Absolutely not!

DEFEATING FEAR

SECTION 3

WE THREE KINGS

"A leader lives with people to know their problems.
A leader lives with God in order to solve them."
John Maxwell

"Where there is no wise guidance, the nation falls, but in the
multitude of counselors there is victory."
Proverbs 11:14

DEFEATING FEAR

SECTION 3 • WE THREE KINGS

6   A Destiny Destroyed

"But am I not a Benjamite, from the smallest tribe of Israel, and is not
my clan the least of all the clans of the tribe of Benjamin?"
1 Samuel 9:21

"A man who wants to lead the orchestra must turn
his back on the crowd."
Max Lucado

The people of the nation were crying out for change. They longed for a leader who would come in as a savior of the land and protect them from all wrong doing and attack. Crying out for a new government, they longed to put their hope in a new messiah. God granted the plea of the people. The cost included higher taxes and total government control. And although fully aware of the price, the people rejoiced.

They had demanded a new leader and their demands were met. The one to lead the nation was an impressive young man. No one rivaled him among the people. Tall in stature and respectable, he honored his family while he cared for their needs. He came from humble beginnings and in his own words he was "once small in his own eyes." He exhibited compassion and valor and he surrounded himself with like-minded, influential people. Certainly, this leader would not bring such destruction to the nation. Change was in the air.

......

Fear caused the men of Israel to demand a king. Their reason was given in 1 Samuel 8:19-20, *"We want a king over us. Then we will be like all the other nations, with a king to lead us and to go out before us and fight our battles."* Fear put the people of Israel at the mercy of a king, and fear brought that very king to his destruction.

God answered the prayers of His people and instructed Samuel to give them a king. The chosen one, Saul, came from the least of the tribes of Israel. He started out his reign with great intentions and a humble heart. As a matter of fact, even after being appointed king over Israel, he could be seen in his father's fields following behind the oxen. His first political move saved the people of Jabesh Gilead from the Ammonites. He did this successfully, and the admiration of the people propelled him into the leadership roll which had been designed just for him.

After Saul began his reign as king, Samuel instructed the people of Israel that if they faithfully walked in the fear of the Lord, they would be blessed and their nation would be protected. Samuel showed the Israelites how greatly they had sinned by replacing God with a king, when he called down rain and thunder from Heaven to destroy the wheat of the fields. This disaster opened the eyes of the people and they repented before their God. Samuel reassured them in 1 Samuel 12:20 as he said, *"Do not be afraid, you have done all this evil; yet, do not turn away from the Lord, but serve the Lord with all your heart."* These words were intended not just for the people of Israel, but for their newly appointed king as well.

SAUL'S DESTINY

God chose Saul to lead Israel. He implanted this destiny within Saul. He anointed Saul for this great mission. Saul only had to obey the commands of God and he and his people would prosper in the land they had been given. To help Saul accomplish this task, God gave him Samuel the prophet to direct and lead him. But even with the ringing of God's very voice in his ears, Saul made two fatal mistakes which would change the course of his life and his destiny forever.

Saul's first mistake was recorded in 1 Samuel 13. Even though God had recently pulled off another miracle for Israel in the beginning of the chapter, we find the Philistine army gathering to come against the Israelites in response to their victory. Saul's men ran for cover. Now, this anointed man of God allowed the *fearfulness of his soldiers* and *the oppressiveness of his enemy* to control and cloud his judgment. He decided to take matters into his own hands. His mind must have been wildly wandering as he impatiently waited for Samuel to meet him at the appointed time and place. King Saul could not reach the Lord for the guidance he desperately needed. With his troops fleeing and Samuel nowhere in sight, he felt abandoned and fearful, so when Samuel did not arrive promptly, Saul made the fatal mistake we have all made at one time or another, he took matters into his own hands. Hastily, Saul prepared a sacrifice for God which by law was a task reserved for a priest, in hopes that God would spare him and his troops. His impatience brought on disobedience, and in that one bad decision, that one act of disobedience, Saul proved he could not be trusted with the authority God had given him.

The Death Blow to Saul's destiny came with his second fatal mistake. The events in Chapter 15 of 1 Samuel show God's way of giving Saul another chance to redeem himself, but what did he do? Again, he not only disobeyed God, but he blamed everyone else for it, he defended his bad decisions, and ultimately, he worried more about his image than he did about his sin. And now let's contemplate this victim excuse. First Samuel 15:24 (AMP) tells us in Saul's own words, *"...I feared the people and obeyed their voice."* Take a moment and let the words of this mighty man of God sink in.

The fear of man destroyed Saul's destiny. The more he feared, the more he ran in the wrong direction. And the more he ran in the wrong direction, the more he played the blame game. Isn't it funny how incredibly victimized we become when we make a bad choice and are faced with the consequences? Fear has led more people to desperation, which then leads to nothing but excuses. Making excuses cost Saul everything. Excuses will keep you from accepting responsibility, and until you can accept responsibility, you will never be ready to step into your destiny. I believe if Saul had taken his failure like a man, if he had repented before God and walked in his anointing, his future would have looked very different.

If you have been carrying around a victim mentality and have been guilty of blaming everyone else for your failure and lack of success, stop now! You will go nowhere with this attitude, and it will hold you hostage. If you are living with a victim mentality then you truly are a victim. You have made yourself one. You are living as a victim of fear. Learn from Saul and break free from the chains that are binding you. Take responsibility for your life. Forgive those who have let you down. Repent for choosing to play the victim and refuse to be held in captivity any longer.

The number one destiny killer is fear, and if fear can destroy the destiny of an anointed and appointed man of God like King Saul, who are we to think we can build our businesses, lead our people, run our homes, raise our kids, lead our countries, shepherd our churches, build our ministries, or save our marriages without totally relying on our Savior?

Take a moment to look at our world. Fear has left devastation and destruction in its wake. What brought the United States to the point of crisis it is in today? The nasty four letter word—FEAR. The fear of losing control of power or of never having power back again. The fear of looking weak financially to the world and to the voters. The fear of criticism from the opposing side of the isle. The fear of being judged if we are not politically correct. I could go on for pages with this one, but I think you get the point.

Think of the dumbest thing you have ever done, and I would guess if you go back to its root, you will find fear lurking. Every stupid business decision I have ever made was made out of fear. At the root of each of those decisions lurked the fear of loss, the fear of missing out, the fear of man, the fear of rejection, and the fear of failure. This is why fear is so widely used among people who need to sell us something. In life we are always facing sales pitches. Our parents sold us on the importance of getting good grades, doing the right thing, and telling the truth. Our teachers sold us on our duty to learn their material and pass their tests. From politicians to teachers and from parents to preachers, fear is an effective sales tool. Turn on your TV for five minutes, and I challenge you to find a news program or a modern TV show that does not capitalize on fear in some way. And if you submit to this kind of entertainment on a regular basis, you will defeat yourself and your destiny. You cannot expect to fill your head with fear and then defeat it at the same time. You cannot live in the enemy camp without being subject to its authority.

If you are depressed, stressed, and oppressed by the current affairs in the world, stop watching and listening to the news regularly. I am not telling you to stick your head in the sand. You need to know what is going on around you, but you do not need to watch and listen to the news several times a day, especially before going to bed. It is just not healthy or profitable.

There is a reason we are instructed to think on *"...whatever is true, whatever is noble, whatever is right, whatever is pure, whatever is lovely, whatever is admirable – if anything is excellent or praiseworthy..."* (Philippians 4:8-9). These thoughts lead to faith, not fear. Saul lived in fear because he thought in fear. The more he feared, the more irrational he became, and instead of dying a hero, he died a fool. Instead of living a life worthy of a king, he spent his kingship hunting down the one man who saved his people, soothed his soul, and loved his son.

King Saul reigned over Israel for forty-two years. In two of those decades, he was responsible for organizing the Israelite tribes so they were able to keep their enemies at bay. He paved the way for King David to expand the kingdom for God's people, but the conflict that waged war within him caused him to be erratic, unstable, and even violent. This great leader of men, this anointed and appointed one of God, lived out his kingship as a tragic prisoner to the spirit of fear within him. And instead of being remembered for his great accomplishments, his legacy is failure.

What if Saul had sought God for wisdom and understanding instead of reacting to his circumstances? Saul lacked the wisdom, knowledge, and understanding of his God, and that lack allowed fear to lead him to reacting. What if he had known that fear was his true enemy? That knowledge of the real enemy mixed with wisdom from the Lord would have given him the power to defeat his foe and fulfill his destiny. And better yet, what if you chose today to learn from Saul's mistakes? What if you were to learn about your enemy so that in times of crisis you would choose to deliver the death blow to him instead of allowing him to destroy your destiny?

Fear is your enemy. Fear will rob you, cheat you, and defeat you. In order to fulfill the destiny you were put here to accomplish, you must develop a faith that far surpasses any fear that threatens to overcome you.

LESSONS LEARNED

There is much to learn from King Saul, and in defense of this fallen man of God, I want to make it a point to reveal the good and the bad lessons from his life.

Lesson 1 – When God calls, answer quickly with obedience. Saul did this in the beginning when God chose him to be king over Israel. Had he remembered this one lesson, his legacy would look very different today.

Lesson 2 – Always defend the little guy, knowing that whatever happens to him could just as easily happen to you. Saul's defense of the people of Jabesh Gilead was a spectacular display of leadership. He rallied the troops, went into battle with them and defended the helpless. That is why, at his death, the ones who defended him and honored him were the very ones he saved forty years earlier.

Lesson 3 – Be patient. *"A man's wisdom gives him patience"* (Proverbs 19:11). Saul's failure came when his patience lacked. God works on *His* timetable not yours. Your faith in Him will be revealed by your patience in all circumstances.

Lesson 4 – The fear of man leads to destruction. A person in leadership will never be effective as long as they are more concerned about man than God. This fear will always, without exception, prove to be a snare. King Saul never learned this lesson and thus destroyed his destiny. When you fear man, you are making him an idol. You are becoming subject to him. But God says we are to be subject to no one but Him alone. The fear of God will propel you into the Promised Land. The fear of man will keep you wandering in the wilderness. It is your choice.

Lesson 5 – *"As a dog returns to its vomit, so a fool repeats his folly"* (Proverbs 26:11). Saul admitted to being a fool, but sadly he remained one. When you realize you have been a fool, repent and ask God to help you change. Admitting your foolishness and not changing is the epitome of foolishness. The change you need can only come from God. In your own strength you may change for a time, but you will inevitably return to your old ways. Repentance before God and dependence on Him to create a new person in you is the only way to find victory in this area.

I am sure that if you take the time to learn about King Saul's life, and I recommend that you do, you will find many more lessons. The life of Saul is an incredible study which has blessed me immensely and has changed my life forever. For those seeking their destiny and purpose, the life of this man is invaluable.

BATTLE STRATEGIES OF A KING

There is much to be learned from a person's battle strategies. In business, we often hear that we will achieve that which we have charted out. If it is not in writing, it will not be in reality. Strategy is critical to victory in battle. This explains why King Saul found defeat and fear when he turned from strategy. Without a strategy, fear has free range to roam. For a mighty warrior of God, none of us want to be in a losing position.

There are several battles to study in the life of King Saul. In the first battle of his career, he met with great success. It was this victory which caused him to gain the trust of the Israelites and placed him on the throne of the kingdom. This was the battle for the people of Jabesh Gilead. Saul's steps were clear, concise, and commanding. He established his authority from the start when he sent a very strong message to the enemy, essentially, "If you are not for us, you are dead." Can't get any clearer than that! Next, he became a leader by rallying the troops. He inspired his warriors, and then separated them into three divisions. Finally, Saul chose to attack the enemy camp at night. The Israelites met with incredible success. A kingdom was now established.

One thing we do not see in the battle for Jabesh Gilead is whether Saul sought God. From what I have read, I see no signs of it, but I also can see where there was no need for it. How can I say that? Some things God has made very clear. God would not allow anyone to come against His people Israel unless their own disobedience caused them to stray from Him. Saul knew his responsibility to protect God's people. He understood his destiny, so when he received the news of the attack on God's chosen ones there should have been no doubt as to how he should respond. And as we learned, there wasn't. In this case, expediency was mandatory.

King Saul showed some wisdom after he took the throne as king. He waited two years before attacking the Philistine army. Was he preparing for the attack during that time? We may never know. If so, it might have been a good idea to find workers to smelt iron, so the fighting men could go into battle with more than pitchforks and farm tools. But nevertheless, Saul decided it was finally time to take down the enemy. In his worldly wisdom, he selected and trained three thousand men. Then he divided the ranks, giving his son Jonathan command over one thousand of them. King Saul must have successfully trained his men for the battle since they were able to wipe out the enemy garrison, but in the process, they stirred up quite a hornets' nest. The Philistine leaders responded swiftly to the boldness of the Israelites by sending an army equipped with chariots, horsemen, and foot soldiers to march on Michmash (not far from Saul's capitol).

Forgetting their recent victories, forgetting what God had done for their people through the generations, forgetting how they had begged for a God-ordained king to protect them, the Israelite army put its tail between its legs and ran to the hills. Overcome with fear, Saul's mighty army went from three thousand to six hundred in a matter of moments. What happened to the mighty, well-trained warriors? Had Saul ever taken the time to remind them of who they were? People of destiny build vision in those around them. Had Saul done that? If he had, would his troops have stayed by his side? If they had rallied to him, would he have still reacted in a way that would cause Samuel to declare, *"But now your kingdom will not endure"*(1 Samuel 13:14)? We will never know.

The final battle with the Amalikites, although not the last in Saul's career, marked the end of his spiritual authority and anointing of God. I really feel this battle was God's last attempt to allow Saul to redeem himself, but in his disobedience once again, he failed his God.

God left no room for failure during this battle. He gave Saul direct orders through Samuel. There were no questions left unanswered. All Saul had to do was go into the city of Amalek, totally destroy everything and spare nothing. The command was straight, simple, and to the point. Even a caveman could understand that. But King Saul took King Agag from the city alive and the army *"spared the best of the sheep and cattle, the fat calves and lambs—everything that was good. They were unwilling to destroy these completely, but everything that was despised and weak they totally destroyed"* (1 Samuel 15:9, emphasis mine). And how did God respond to their disobedience? *"I am grieved that I have made Saul king, because he has turned away from me and has not carried out my instructions"* (v.11).

Has God been leading you to do something, give something, or destroy something which you have been unwilling to do? Have you felt led to give something you didn't want to give, or to destroy a stronghold which has been holding you back? Many times, the very thing which will keep you from your destiny is your unwillingness to submit all to your Savior. It is work to step into God's purpose for your life, but it is worth it. Taking a stand in a dark world isn't always fun, but the promises that accompany the obedience are priceless. The Israelites allowed their greed to dictate their disobedience. Have you? God seeks obedience and abhors rebellion.

While God and Samuel mourned over King Saul's lack of leadership, the king walked in pride. He thought he had done a fine job for God, so much so that when Samuel went to rebuke him, he found Saul in Carmel putting up a monument, not for his God mind you, but for his own honor! You know the end of the story. Saul was a victim of fear. When Samuel rebuked him, there was no sign of repentance, just more pride as Saul begged Samuel to be seen with him before the people.

Fear, pride, arrogance, lack of repentance, disobedience, victim mentality, excuses, and blame. In a nutshell, these words represent the reign of King Saul prior to the arrival of David. And much like the spoiled child who never seems to learn a lesson, things do not get better from here.

So what do we learn from Saul's battle strategies? When he had one and he followed it, he had success. When he had one and didn't follow it, he failed miserably and destroyed his destiny.

How does this affect your life today? Can you see a bit of Saul in the way you are living? What one thing can you take away from the life of Saul and apply to your life now so that you will be known as one who walks in obedience before your God? Take a moment to record it on the next page before you read further.

If there were not so many lessons to learn from King Saul, this chapter could have been depressing, but his life is challenging and encouraging for those looking to grow into greatness. Fortunately, the next two kings we are going to study, although still subject to fear at times, trusted God more and thus found the ultimate victory.

DEFEATING FEAR

SECTION 3 • WE THREE KINGS

7   A Destiny Leader

*"We demolish arguments and every pretension that sets itself up
against the knowledge of God, and we take captive every
thought to make it obedient to Christ."*
2 Corinthians 10:5

*"Courage is contagious. When a brave man takes a stand,
the spines of others are stiffened."*
Billy Graham

Things had been pretty easy the first four years of this young boy's life. He lacked nothing. Any wish he had was his for the taking. His future was bright, until…

One day while crawling around the floor of his father's office in search of the missing piece to his toy, he heard the bleak report. An army not far off prepared to attack the nation. The enemy outnumbered them two to one, but in the midst of the fear-enveloped room, he heard his father cry out, *"O Lord, there is none besides You to help, and it makes no difference to You whether the one You help is mighty or powerless. Help us, O Lord our God! For we rely on You, and we go against this multitude in Your name. O Lord, You are our God; let no man prevail against You!"* (2 Chronicles 14:11).

With that one simple, faith filled prayer, his father headed off to face the enemy while the small child wondered if he would ever see his daddy again.

......

No one will ever know if that is an accurate depiction of the early events of Jehoshaphat's life, but one thing we do know for sure is that early in his career his father, King Asa, was a great strategist and military commander as king of Judah. Is it any wonder then that Jehoshaphat grew to be such a great leader, a lover of God and a battle-ready warrior? His father had taught him well, and he learned from the best. It makes us stop and wonder what our kids, grandkids, nieces, nephews, or siblings are learning from us, doesn't it?

King Asa loved God, and he expressed that love for his Lord in words and in deeds (2 Chronicles 14:2-5), so in God's good pleasure, He blessed Judah with peace for the first ten years of Asa's reign.

King Asa walked in wisdom during that time as he not only strengthened his nation, but he groomed its next king as well. We can all learn from and apply his strategy for war as we come out against approaching armies determined to destroy our destinies. It was quite simple.

1. Build and secure your walls during times of peace.
2. Be prepared for battle at all times. *"...be prepared in season and out of season"* (2 Timothy 4:2)
3. Train and raise up mighty men (and women) of courage.
4. When the enemy approaches, set up a firm line of defense.
5. Cry out to the Lord for direction BEFORE the battle begins.

Do you think Jehoshaphat had any idea what he was learning from his father during that time? Probably not, but the events that led up to that battle, and the ones that followed must have permeated the recesses of his young mind because years later, Jehoshaphat would apply and expand on what he learned from his father's fine example.

*** WARNING ***
COMPLACENCY AFTER VICTORY
BRINGS DEATH TO DESTINY!!!

When are you most likely to whine? When things have been going badly and something else happens? Or is it when life has been rolling along at a leisurely pace, everything is perfect and BAM! Then it is, "Why me? Why does everything happen to me? Why is the world against me? Why, why, why????" Oddly enough, it is usually the latter. When this happens, the explanation is easy. You have become a victim of complacency. The battle you walked courageously through previously is now a distant memory. You have let down your guard. You have fallen for the lie that you are somehow in control. Unfortunately, just as we see with King Asa in 2 Chronicles 16, complacency often brings with it a form of worship, but not of Almighty God. No! The one we often place on the altar of our tabernacle is none other than *ourselves*.

After thirty years of peace and prosperity, King Asa grew a bit spoiled. His zeal for God must have gotten lost in his comfort because when Baasha king of Israel threatened to come against the nation of Judah, King Asa forgot his own successful battle plan! He could have written the book *The Idiot's Guide to Battle Strategy*. He knew the blessings which followed such wisdom—his nation had benefited from it for thirty years—but somewhere along the way, he forgot. Complacency will blind you.

In fear, King Asa took matters into his own hands. This man who sought God for his nation, taught God to his people, and had done *"what was good and right in the eyes of the Lord his God,"* (2 Chronicles 14:2) shrunk back and subjected himself to one whom he perceived was mightier than he. As quickly as he could, he robbed the treasuries of the Lord's temple, gathered all of the valuables from his own palace, cashed in his IRA, sold his stocks, and mortgaged his home, putting his trust in man and not God. The plan worked for a moment. Those plans usually do, but....

Do they really work? Decisions made out of fear become decisions made out of desperation. Don't put yourself in such a dangerous place when your future is on the line. In moments of panic, it's easy not to think about the consequences of the decisions. Borrowing against the house will put you in greater debt. Cashing in the IRAs will empty your retirement accounts and make it necessary for you to work another fifteen years. Declaring bankruptcy will destroy not just your credit but your credibility. But, there is no time to think of that now because you must do something! Right? Wrong!

King Asa fell into the same trap man still finds himself ensnared in today. In complacency, we have no need for God. In complacency, we fall for the lie that man can help me, the government will fix it, my boss will take care of me, and my spouse will make me happy. Asa no doubt had great relationships with other leaders, which is why he felt confident enough to neglect God and go fix the problem on his own.

So why all of this talk about King Asa in a chapter which is supposed to be about his son? Because Asa had an outstanding career for the first thirty-six years of his forty-one year reign, and paved the way for the great leadership Jehoshaphat displayed in his career. But fear and complacency did something to him from which we all need to learn. King Asa became arrogant, dependent on man, unrepentant, and brutal in the last five years on the throne of Judah. He lost sight of the God he had once lovingly served because he got comfortable. Records do not indicate that he lost children, or that God treated the nation of Judah harshly during that time. On the contrary, the Bible states the opposite. King Asa and the nation of Judah were blessed during his leadership. He forsook the laws he had lived by early on, and for that mistake, he spent the remainder of his life at war.

King Asa forgot about the character of God in his final years upon this earth. Fear will do that. The good news is that for the majority of the King's life, he loved his God and that is the father Jehoshaphat appears to recall during his reign.

CRUSHED BUT NOT DESTROYED

Hard pressed on every side—we have all been there at one time or another. Maybe you are there right now. There were cut backs at work, and you were one of the first to go. You could find a position in another state, but the home you can no longer afford is not selling. The bank calls every hour to make threats of foreclosure if you do not get current with your mortgage. The kids have dental bills, the oil needs to be changed, the suit you need for your job interview remains at the cleaner because when you scrounged around the house looking for change, you came up $2.00 short. And as if that's not enough already, the washer just broke down with your son's soccer uniform for the game tonight inside and water spilled onto your hardwood floor! You are pressed down.

King Jehoshaphat knew the feeling of being hard pressed on every side when his men dashed into his palace with the news that a vast army marched against him and the people of Judah. Jehoshaphat's first response was that of fear. What else could any person feel in a moment like that, but what he did next is what set him apart, and if you apply this wisdom, it will set you apart too. The Amplified Bible says it so perfectly in 2 Chronicles 20:3, *"Then Jehoshaphat feared, and set himself [determinedly, as his vital need] to seek the Lord; he proclaimed a fast in all Judah."*

THE BATTLE STRATEGY

Fear was pressing in on him. He had a kingdom depending on him to protect them. But in the heat of the moment when I am sure he wanted to take control and fix everything, he chose to seek God. He chose to trust God over man. I wonder if he remembered in those heart-stopping seconds while fear knocked at his door, that vital moment when his father submitted his nation before God. As this vast army appeared just beyond the walls of his city, I am sure he fought the temptation to take charge, to order people to do something, anything. But when it mattered most, the king of Judah called his people to stop, pray, and fast so they could hear from God. And the people of Judah obeyed because the leader of their nation was a man of great faith. Fear may sell in the marketplace, but faith will draw people to you like the beautiful, ripe fruit of August attracts every fruit fly in the State of Washington to my home each year. And King Jehoshaphat, by demonstrating his faith, became a leader worth following. His strategy in this battle was not only powerfully simple, but it is also one to be documented, studied, memorized, and put into practice in the battle for your destiny.

And it is as simple as this:

1. Seek God through prayer and fasting.
2. Remind God of who He is and what He has done.
3. Admit your dependence on Him.
4. Stand firm.
5. Worship Him before and after battle.

When I discovered these steps, I was breathless. The simplicity of faith as compared to the complexity of fear took me aback. How much more effective could you be as you overcome the paralysis of fear and learn and to implement these powerful steps? They will change your life forever if you apply them to every decision you make from this time on. I guarantee it!

Seeking God in prayer is something many people do readily and easily when trouble hits, but notice how King Jehoshaphat prayed. He starts out with, *"O Lord, God of our fathers, are you not God in heaven?"* (2 Chronicles 20:6). He goes on to give God a list of the many things He has done for the descendants of Abraham. He prays for seven verses before he even mentions their very pressing plight, and when he does you do not find this faithful king begging. Instead, he prays honestly before his God when he says, *"For we have no might to stand against this great company that is coming against us. We do not know what to do, but our eyes are upon You"* (v.12).

God knows the fears you face. He knows the mountains you need to climb. He sees the challenges confronting you. But He created you to be a believer, not a beggar. When you tell Him who He is and what He has done, it is not because He needs to be reminded. It is because *you* need to be reminded. Your faith will grow when you meditate on the character of God. And as your faith grows in the presence of your praise, the fears that taunt you will melt away, and you will hear from Heaven.

WORSHIP IS YOUR WARSHIP

"Stand up and bless the LORD your God, forever and ever!
Blessed be Your glorious name, which is exalted above all blessing and
praise! You alone are the LORD; You have made heaven,
The heaven of heavens, with all their host, The earth and everything
on it, The seas and all that is in them, And You preserve them all.
The host of heaven worships You."
Nehemiah 9:5-6

There are a lot of great people of faith in the Word of God, but I chose to discuss King Jehoshaphat for a reason. His leadership led people to worship, and by leading people to worship, he led a nation to the throne room of God. When he called his people to pray, fast, and seek God, they gathered together, yearning for Him with all of their desire. When is the last time you yearned for God? That yearning for your Savior, the One who bled and died for you, should double you over and bring you to your knees before this God who hears your prayers and heals your land.

When Jehoshaphat heard the answer to the prayers of Judah, he *"bowed his head with his face to the ground, and all Judah and the inhabitants of Jerusalem fell down before the Lord, worshiping him"* (2 Chronicles 20:18). But they didn't stop there. The people worshiped when the Lord gave them an answer, and they worshiped on the way to the battle which they never had to fight, and they worshiped after the victory. Whether they were on their faces before Him, or singing praises to Him as they entered into battle, or whether they were coming into Jerusalem with harps, lyres, and trumpets as they proceeded to the house of the Lord, the people of Judah worshiped their King. They didn't need to plan an event. They didn't take a vote to see if everyone agreed. They didn't check to see whether everyone was in the mood. It was not announced, they didn't even include food, since they were fasting. They just worshiped.

That worship that we seem to neglect in our complacency was the very thing that caused the Lord to *"set ambushes against the men of Ammon, Moab and Mount Seir who were invading Judah, and they were defeated."* (2 Chronicles 20:22). The praises of God's people caused the enemies of God's people to turn against themselves, and the people of God didn't even lift a finger, just a voice.

There is power in worship. It will make the Devil tremble and the demons scatter. A voice lifted to God and a knee bowed to Him will do more damage on the battlefield for your dreams than any skillful plan you could ever conjure up. There is nothing mightier to God than a mighty warrior of the Most High on their knees, prostrate or dancing before Him with reckless abandon because of who He is and what He does.

King Jehoshaphat felt the fear of his world crumbling around him, but his faith was stronger. He knew his God. He remembered His character. And he trusted Him to be who He said He was. Will you?

DEFEATING FEAR

SECTION 3 · WE THREE KINGS

8   A Man after God's Own Heart

"...who is this uncircumcised Philistine that he should
defy the armies of the living God?"
1 Samuel 17:26

"It is not the critic who counts...not the man who points out how the
strong man stumbled, or where the doer of deeds could have done better.
The credit belongs to the man who is actually in the arena; whose face is
marred by dust and sweat and blood; who strives valiantly; who errs
and comes short again and again; who knows the great enthusiasms,
the great devotions and spends himself in a worthy course; who,
at the best, knows in the end the triumph of great achievement,
and who, at worst, if he fails, at least fails while daring greatly;
so that his place shall never be with those cold and timid souls
who know neither victory or defeat."
Theodore Roosevelt

The brunt of all family jokes, the small lad became a target for all the torment his big brothers could dish out. He probably sought the peace and quiet of aloneness. When he escaped into the great outdoors, he felt somehow... *bigger*. In the quietness of nature, he sang, practiced hitting targets and just talked to God. In that solitude, he found his comfort, and since no one seemed to miss him, he often lingered in the tranquility which evaded him at home. But one day, he lingered too long.

••••••

Imagine how David must have felt when the prophet Samuel visited Bethlehem and invited his father, Jesse, and *all* his sons to be consecrated and join him in a sacrifice. Yet no one even thought to summon David, the youngest of them all. At least not until Samuel questioned Jesse. Then as if David were an afterthought, Jesse told him there was one more son out tending the sheep. Talk about being overlooked. This would be the last time in David's life that anyone would ignore him, because Samuel was on a secret mission to anoint the new king of Israel, and this small, ruddy, ridiculed David would be that man—"a man after God's own heart."

How could God choose this insignificant boy for such important work? There were others more qualified, better looking, more talented, and maybe even more intelligent, yet God chose David. And in the same way and for the same reason, God has chosen you. David had a destiny, so do you. David was put here for a purpose and so are you. David loved God passionately, yet often failed him and so will you. David stood up to giants, fought off armies, and established his destiny out of his faith in God. Will you?

FIVE SMOOTH STONES

Fear has an interesting way of giving power to people, circumstances, and situations which in themselves would be and should be powerless. King Saul's kingdom made fear the cornerstone. The people of Israel feared enemy attacks and wanted a king over them, so God gave them their request. That root of fear established itself in King Saul's reign as he made one bad decision after another out of fear.

The Philistine army might have been powerful by earthly standards, but God enabled the Israelite army to defeat them on numerous occasions. Yet we find God's people coming face-to-face with this great contender once again, and as if on cue, they feared.

The Philistines had more than weapons, chariots, vast armies, and equipped soldiers. Yes, they had Goliath of Gath. The very mention of his name made knees weak and hearts fail. The sight of his presence caused grown men to flee and hide. This giant stood over nine feet tall with armor covering him from head to foot.

"He had a bronze helmet on his head and wore a coat of scale armor of bronze weighing five thousand shekels, on his legs he wore bronze greaves, and a bronze javelin was slung on his back. His spear shaft was like a weaver's rod, and its iron point weighed six hundred shekels."
1 Samuel 17:5-7

Can you imagine coming face-to-face with this terrorizing figure? Just to help you understand the enormity of this giant, consider that his armor and spear point alone weighed over 140 pounds! What if a figure like that taunted you for forty days and forty nights, never giving you a moment's rest? What if he mocked you, teased you, stole your sleep, and robbed your peace? What if he kept you a prisoner on a hillside with no sign of relenting? If you have allowed fear to control you, then you know this feeling, because Goliath is a representation of your spiritual condition in the natural form. He represents all fear everywhere. Fear is overwhelming, gigantic, threatening, and relentless. If fear has robbed you of sleep, then you can probably relate with the men of Israel.

David longed to go to war against the Philistine army, but everyone said he was too small and too young. He remained at home dutifully caring for the sheep while his brothers defended God's nation. He had already been anointed by Samuel. He already knew his destiny. And the Spirit of God was already upon him. Yet youthful David continued to honor his earthly father by tending his sheep. He did not spend his time idly waiting for the throne, but he developed his skills for the task ahead. In this humble position, David learned to care for, fight for, and protect his father's flock, so that as he stepped into his destiny, he could shepherd God's flock effectively.

The day finally came when Jesse sent David to deliver supplies to the camp and to bring back a good report about his brothers. David reached the camp just when the army marched out to its battle positions. His heart leapt with excitement as the war cry of the nation rang throughout the battlefield. There he stood in the midst of thousands of mighty men of valor, and he, just a lowly shepherd boy. Oh, to be one of them, a warrior of the Holy One of Israel. As the battle line grew closer, David's excitement got the better of him and he ran out to greet his brothers. As they talked, David heard a booming voice come from behind him. He turned to discover a looming figure standing boldly just beyond the enemy's line. His mouth dropped at the sight of such a man. He heard the words booming from the lips of the Philistine, *"This day I defy the ranks of Israel! Give me a man and let us fight each other."* (1 Samuel 17:10)

David turned toward the warriors on the battlefield, and he was aghast. Not because of the giant, but because the mighty men of valor shook and quaked in their armor. These men of God fled from Goliath in great fear. David thought, *"Who is this uncircumcised Philistine that he should defy the armies of the living God?"* (1 Samuel 17:26).

David trusted the truth of God's Word. Through the outpouring of his faith, David proclaimed that he would fight the giant. Can't you hear the laughter which must have echoed throughout the camp? This little shepherd boy thinks he can go up against that mighty giant? Go home, child, and leave the men here to shrink back in fear before this intimidating foe.

It does not take long for word to get out when a person takes a courageous stand. It is an admired character trait, but one so seldom displayed, so when it is, even the king will hear about it. This was the case with David. King Saul got word that there was a man willing to fight the giant, so he summoned him to his tent. One look at the boy, and King Saul replied, *"You are not able to go out against this Philistine and fight him; you are only a boy, and he has been a fighting man from his youth."* (1 Samuel 17:33). David refused to be denied, and proclaimed to the king, *"Your servant has killed both the lion and the bear; this uncircumcised Philistine will be like one of them, because he has defied the armies of the living God."* (1 Samuel 17:36). Sold, to the insane boy with a death wish upon his head!

THE ARMOR EXCHANGE

This next part of the story always makes me laugh because of the lunacy of it all. King Saul stood a head taller than anyone else in the land. This big guy might not rival Goliath, but tall he towered nonetheless. Saul shopped in the Big and Tall stores, while David still wore junior sizes. But none of these obvious facts influenced King Saul's next offer.

Saul insisted on dressing David in his armor—his personal, individual, custom-made armor! The size difference between King Saul and David made it impossible for David to even move while wearing the king's personal line of warrior wear. David wisely and politely thanked the king for his generosity. Then he chose his familiar weapon—the one he used with deadly accuracy—his sling and five stones.

How many times have you tried to wear the armor of another? Have you tried to dress like, act like, preach like, parent like, or do business like someone else? Most have, and most will continue until they discover their own destiny. David knew who he was and Whose he was, so he could boldly step into his destiny. By the end of this book, you will too!

When people think of fearlessness, David's name often comes to mind. David possessed the courageous heart of a warrior, but he was not fearless. If he were fearless, I believe David would have picked up only one stone, but he didn't. He picked up five. Why? Maybe he thought he should be prepared. He might not hit his target the first time. He knew his record better than anyone else. He had taken on bears and lions and lived to tell about it, but how many times had he missed?

I think the other reason, and the most important one of all, was to inspire us, those of us in the future who would read this incredible story of victory, hope, faith, and courage and find peace and strength in it. When we are stepping up to giants on the battlefields of life, we may need to cast more than one stone. We may need to cast one hundred or even one thousand to receive our victory. The fact that David picked up five stones encourages us in our failures and reminds us to keep the faith, pick up another stone and try again.

David was not fearless. All you need to do is read the Psalms he wrote to discover that fear plagued him throughout his life. What David had going for him is what you will have going for you as you continue to seek God for your destiny. It is simply this: David had more faith than he had fear. Why? Because he knew who he was, Whose he was, and why he was here. That knowledge gave him the power to go boldly against anything which stood in the way of his destiny.

Can you imagine what the army snickered about David as he prepared for battle? His brothers had already condemned him and called him conceited. Jealousy flared amongst them. Yet I am sure as David walked toward Goliath, they must have thought that this would be the last time they would see him alive. David paid no attention to what was being said to him or about him; he just focused on what God had placed before him to do.

Goliath stood in the way of not just David's destiny but of the nation of Israel's destiny too. David had no doubts as he walked out onto the battlefield that day. Where the army saw Goliath in relation to themselves and trembled, David saw Goliath in relation to God and triumphed. In one swift move, a single, perfectly shaped stone propelled across the battlefield which stood between David and his death. It found the one opening in Goliaths spectacular armor, entered in and penetrated his skull, taking the giant to the ground.

David emerged from the battlefield that day a champion. What man had feared, David faced, and with his swift action, he stepped boldly into his destiny.

LESSONS FROM A CHAMPION

There are so many lessons to learn from David's life. I guess that is why there are so many books written about him. His life is inspiring, his successes as well as his mistakes are memorable, and he established the nation of Israel in a powerful way. But this is a book on fear, so I will do my best to keep my focus there.

So what lessons do we learn from David's life?

1. David feared, but his faith was greater than his fear.
2. David prepared himself for his destiny.
3. As long as his eyes were on God, David met with great success.
4. David turned off the world around him to hear God.
5. David did all he could do and then trusted God to save him.

As I said there are many more great lessons from the life of David, and I will touch on some of them throughout the next few chapters, but these five are the ones that inspire me most. I pray they will do the same for you too.

DAVID'S BATTLE STRATEGY

For another thirteen years, David met with battle after battle before he finally took the throne as king of Israel. As king, he spent much of his time defending God's people, establishing His kingdom and advancing against the enemy. His very simple battle strategy served him well when he used it. It involved only three steps, but these three steps are full of power and carry with them great success. Here they are:

1. David talked to God.
2. David got his strategy from God.
3. David went into battle.

That's it. David completely depended on God. David relied on the loving voice of his Father to lead him through the challenges carried with his destiny. The two times in David's life when he willfully turned away from God brought David's greatest failures in his own eyes. These two times of sin and separation were the most depressing times of David's life. During these twelve- and sixteen-month periods, he penned no Psalms. Once he returned to his God, his strategy returned to the simplicity of its original form. Talk to God, listen and wait for his strategy, and then enter into battle.

Are you going through one of those times, when there are no psalms coming from your pen, no prayers coming from your lips, and fear has overshadowed your faith? Are you willing to stay in the fight for your destiny and give it one more chance? Then surrender your heart to the God Who created you for a purpose. David did after one of his greatest failures. When his men prepared to stone him after finding their homes burned and their families taken captive, he finally looked up again, and *"found strength in the Lord his God"* (1 Samuel 30:6). While his six hundred warriors stoked their anger against him, David rekindled the fire in his heart for his God. David listened to God's leading and miraculously rallied his once disgruntled troops, captured the enemy, and recovered everything that had been taken from them. David discovered a universal truth—if you seek God with all of your heart you will find Him. If you have drifted far from God, He has not been far from you. If your enemy fear is oppressing you like Goliath, taunting you day and night, will you seek God as David did? If you said yes, then prepare for battle, because we are going in!

DEFEATING FEAR

SECTION 4

OVERCOMING THE PARALYSIS OF FEAR

*"Fear not [there is nothing to fear], for I am with you; do not look
around you in terror and be dismayed, for I am your God.
I will strengthen and harden you to difficulties, yes, I will help you;
yes, I will hold you up and retain you with My [victorious]
right hand of rightness and justice."*
Isaiah 41:10 (AMP)

*"You gain strength, courage, and confidence by every experience
in which you really stop to look fear in the face."*
Eleanor Roosevelt

When it comes to overcoming fear, you can find all kinds of interesting ideas. These strategies have supplied me with many hours of
comic relief, and I thought that by now, you could use a little levity too!

Of course, we have the old standby that fear is simply false evidence appearing real. That may contain some truth, but there are many
fears that simply are real. Imagine that you are out on a lovely walk in
the evening and suddenly a large grizzly bear comes upon your path.
No false evidence here! Now you have two choices, you can become

paralyzed and do nothing or you can use your brain and do something. I would recommend doing something, since doing nothing will surely cause you to end up being the main course in this bear's dinner!

Perhaps you have heard about spelling out your fear with your favorite bite sized food and eating it. Now you are not only living in fear, but you will probably gain ten pounds in the process. Being a health coach, I do not recommend this one.

Another idea recommends writing your fear on a piece of paper and torching the fear thereby getting rid of it. Okay, since fear of fire often tops the list of fears, I would say that this one may not be the best idea either, and if I were a betting woman, I would bet that after the process, you would still have the fear and maybe a house fire too! If you do want to try this one, please have your fire extinguisher ready.

One last one before I get onto more constructive ideas is to write your fear on paper and then cut up the paper into a million pieces and throw it away. This one is quite helpful for those who fear fire. Of course, with the recent green movement, this may not be a viable option for you.

I am always amazed to hear the list of top fears. Number one is the fear of public speaking. Number two is the fear of snakes. And I heard number three was the fear of speaking to a room full of snakes!

All kidding aside, no matter what the fear, it still comes down to the same thing. If you do nothing, the fear will remain and will gain in intensity. If you take steps to eradicate your fear, you may not always be victorious, but your life will be more successful, and you will learn not to be controlled by that little four letter word called fear.

You have been going through a lot of self-discovery prior to this last section, but throughout the process, you have been preparing yourself to take action. Each exercise in this book is designed to equip you for battle. Each previous step has placed you that much closer to accomplishing that which you were put here to do. Remember, you were put here for a purpose. The time is now to pick up your stones and step into the battle!

You are a mighty warrior of the Most High God! Welcome to the front lines!

DEFEATING FEAR

SECTION 4 • OVERCOMING THE
PARALYSIS OF FEAR

9   F is for Fight

*"...you are approaching the battle against your enemies today.
Do not be faint-hearted. Do not be afraid, or panic, or tremble before
them, for the Lord your God is the one who goes with you,
to fight for you against your enemies, to save you."*
Deuteronomy 20:3-4

*"Courage faces fear and thereby masters it;
cowardice represses fear and is thereby mastered by it."*
Martin Luther King, Jr.

If you want to truly overcome the paralysis of fear, you must be aggressive and fight. Fear is a spiritual enemy at war within your life with the sole purpose of destroying your destiny. You only have one way to come out against it, and that is with fists flying.

Without a fight, fear will reign over your thoughts, bringing with it discouragement, doubt, and guilt. If you fail to stand up and fight, you will surely experience defeat. And when I say fight, I mean to fight with everything you have inside. To take down this giant, you will need to give it everything you've got. The more you do this, the easier it will become because with each victory, you will gain the confidence you need to believe you can do it again.

The most important part of the fighting process is to simply put your foot on the battlefield. That may seem like nothing to you, but the pathway to success is taken one step at a time. And that is how this war for your destiny will succeed. Wars are won a battle at a time. God told Moses to take the land little by little. He actually said to Moses in Deuteronomy 7:22, *"You will not be allowed to eliminate them all at once, or the wild animals will multiply all around you."* In other words, God told Moses to be patient, yet persistent, and in the process, God warned him not to get ahead of himself lest he be eaten by the wild animals! We are not to despise small beginnings. When we do, we set ourselves up for challenges we may not be able to handle just yet. Be prepared to take the land one battle at a time. But first things first, if you do not get your feet onto the battlefield, you will not be part of the fight.

As a fighter, you are going out there to battle, to contend, to crusade, and to strive to overcome. You are striving to overcome the paralysis of fear. What I found interesting in researching the word fight is that its opposite is to fear. So when you choose to fight for your destiny, you are opposing fear and standing in faith.

It isn't always easy to fight. There will be times when you will want to pull the covers over your head and hide, but that is when your faith needs to be bigger than your fear. Don't expect to feel confident, to feel good or to feel strong. This is not about feelings; this is about faith. Have faith in who you are, in Whose you are, and in what your purpose is in being here, and you will march boldly onto the battlefield knowing this was a fight laid out for you.

But how do you know when to fight? Not *every* fight is for you. You do not need to climb every mountain. Many times, trying to forge the rushing river of someone else's dream prevents you from forging your own. This is where the first section of the book comes into play.

You will know when to fight and where to invest your time based on your destiny. Trust God to lead you in this. Trust Him to direct your steps. Just as He led Moses, Joshua, Samuel, David, Ester, Paul, and countless others, He will lead you too. I am not instructing you to be selfish or to think only of yourself here. Actually, what I am telling you is quite the opposite. I am exhorting you to live out the life God laid out for you before the beginning of time, and when you do that, you will serve His people, express His love, inspire others, and bring Him glory.

THE HEART OF A CHAMPION

"Courage is when you're scared to death, but you saddle up anyway."
John Wayne

Remember the Rocky movies? They exuded inspiration. This penniless man is past his prime as a fighter, and has squandered his life working as a thug for a Philadelphia lone shark. He wants something more, but he believes the lie he has been told his whole life. The lie that he is nothing and will never be anything. But one day, fate comes knocking on his door. Rocky had a dream to be a fighter, and Apollo Creed was looking for an opponent he knew he could beat. He chose a nobody off the streets of nowhere to contend against him for the title of Heavyweight Champion of the World. But in choosing Rocky, he made one fatal mistake. Apollo Creed handpicked a man with a great need, a big dream, and an unquenchable spirit.

Rocky worked hard to prepare for the fight of his life. He sacrificed, he suffered, and he surrendered for this chance of a lifetime. Rocky intended not to win the fight but to give it his best. He wanted to leave nothing out of the ring. He knew it would be painful. He knew it would be exhausting. And he knew he could, and probably would lose to the Champion. But in Rocky's mind, being a failure was more about giving up than losing. So with everything he had inside and the intention to go the distance with the Champion, Rocky stepped into the ring, and he took on the giant.

Rocky did not win that fight, but he did stay in the ring the entire fifteen rounds. He made history. He stepped into his destiny and a warrior was born.

You may be saying that Rocky was a fictional character, and that is true, but Rocky lives in the heart and soul of all of us. The Rocky movies were created to express the heart of a fighter. They were created to give hope to the underdog, to encourage people to believe that they can be better than they are today, and to give them permission again to dream. These movies remind us that when we are knocked down, we have the ability to get back up again. They teach us that it doesn't matter what others say about us, it only matters what we believe.

Inside each of us is the heart of a fighter. The reason so many of us relate with Rocky is because everyone at some time or another has been in the ring with a bigger, smarter, and more capable opponent. Many of us have either slithered out of the ring living to regret it, or we have been pulverized and stopped because of shame and embarrassment. Few have stayed in the ring to fight against all odds and have come out the champion. But far too many have allowed fear to keep them out of the ring altogether, and they spend their lives as spectators, choosing instead to watch from the safety of the bleachers as others triumph or fall on their faces.

The fight for your destiny will require that you have the heart of a champion. Others may mock you, criticize you, and try to convince you to give up before you start, but God has something different to say to you. God says that you were fearfully and wonderfully made in His image, and that if you go about the great task of living out your destiny, He will never leave your side. He knows the battles you will fight. He knows who will come against you, but He also knows that He is God and His Word is final. What others intend for harm, God will use for good. What was meant for your destruction, God will use to strengthen you. There is nothing beyond His reach or ability, but He is looking for warriors who can enter the fight with an unshakable faith not in themselves but in their God and in His promises.

WARRIORS WANTED

"These things I have spoken to you, so that in Me you may have peace.
In the world you will have tribulation, but take courage;
I have overcome the world."
John 16:33 (NASB)

What does God look for in a fighter? He looks for someone who is not faint-hearted. What does He expect from the warriors who take their battle positions? He expects men and woman who do not become complacent in times of peace. Are there guidelines in His Word which will reveal the truth of His expectations? Absolutely! Throughout His Word, you will find examples of people who lived according to God's expectations of a fighter, but in Deuteronomy 20, you will find a list of His expectations and among this list, there are several great lessons to learn.

Lesson number one is found in Deuteronomy 20:1, *"When you go to war against your enemies and see horses and chariots and an army great-*

er than yours…" It is not if, but WHEN you go to war. Somewhere along the way, there has been a new mantra in our Christian culture which says believers should never experience trials on this earth. This is a lie. The truth is believers will experience all kinds of trials but can rest in the comfort of knowing that their future rests in God's loving, caring hands. Everything you experience in this life will be used for your growth and ultimately His glory. You are not subject to the lies and lures of the evil one unless you choose to hear his voice over the whisper of your Savior. Trials will come, but when they do….

Do not be afraid of them, because the Lord your God…will be with you" (Deuteronomy 20:1). Lesson number two—do not be afraid because God is always with you. Your security as a Christian has nothing to do with having a great security system, a closet full of guns, or a mighty fortress for your family. I can't emphasize this enough. *The Lord your God will be with you.* That's His promise, so fear not, because God is your supply. Fear not, because the same God who brought the Israelites out of Egypt is the God who is with you now. There is nothing too big, no mountain too tall, no enemy too strong, no problem too difficult, no marriage too far gone, no child too rebellious, and no sin too great. The God who created the universe can and will supply whatever His army needs.

Finally, in Deuteronomy 20:5-8 (KJV), we are given a clear description of who is fit, or rather, who is unfit for battle. *"Has anyone built a new house and not dedicated it?…Has anyone planted a vineyard and not begun to use its fruit?"* In other words, is your home in order? Have your fields been prepared for harvest? The battles will come, so in times of peace, prepare. The kicker comes in verse 8, which is worthy of being read in its entirety, *"Then the officers shall speak further to the people, and they shall say, 'Who is the man that is afraid and fainthearted? Let him depart and return to his house, so that he might not make his brothers' hearts melt like his heart.'* Fear is contagious. Fear will make you double-minded, and you cannot go into battle and experience victory unless your focus is clear. People walking in fear were not considered worthy of battle, and it was known that they caused others to fall into fear also, so they were sent home. Where do you stand? Is your home in order? Have you tended your provisions? Are you walking in faith? Yes? Then step out in faith, for the battle is the Lord's.

······

Long before Saul feared, Jehoshaphat worshiped, or David took down a giant, there was a man of courage named Joshua who had the honor of leading God's people into the Promised Land. After forty years of wandering in the wilderness, fear had kept the Israelites on the outside of God's promises looking in. At last the time had come, the victory was sure, the good life was just around the corner, or so they thought. Just like many of us, the Israelites liked the idea of God's promises but not the fact that they had to actually work for them. This attitude kept God's people wandering aimlessly for forty years, and today, far too often, it continues to be the attitude in the church.

The book of Joshua teaches the courage necessary for fighting for God's promises. The Israelites, who were expecting to waltz in and easily take over, had to fight for their Promised Land, and you will need to fight for yours too. They had to believe God would help them to conquer the enemies who stood between them and their destiny, and you will too. Throughout the entire first chapter of Joshua, God feels the need to remind Joshua to be courageous. In fact, in the first ten verses of chapter 1, God tells him four times to "be strong and courageous." Why? Because God knew what it was going to take for man to boldly live out his destiny. He knew that when you lived out your purposes, He would be glorified and the enemy would be angry. This was true for Joshua too.

To equip you for victory, God implanted within the Word for Joshua and for you today, a seven step process for guaranteed success in battle. The steps are simple yet ignored by many but not by Joshua, and after today, I pray not by you either. They are so simple, in fact, that they do not even need any further explanation. Just read and apply.

Laws of Success for Joshua:

1. Listen to God. (Joshua 1:2)
2. Obey Him without hesitation.(Joshua 1 :2)
3. Trust God. (Joshua 1:5)
4. Be courageous. (Joshua 1:6)
5. Keep God's commands. (Joshua 1:7)
6. Study His Word daily. (Joshua 1:8)
7. Be not afraid. (Joshua 1:9)

After hearing from God, Joshua stepped into action. He didn't need to confirm it with anyone or to get the opinions of the people. He just took God at His word and gave the orders to the officers for the Israelites. The first command was to get your supplies ready. You will want to check your inventory before stepping out also. What tools has God given you?

What are your supplies? Every warrior adequately equipped for battle has supplies, and you will too if you are going to have half of a chance on the battlefield. First up is your armor.

Remember when we discussed the value of being dressed in the full armor of God in the faith chapter? This is where you will need it. Remember that each piece of armor is necessary and mandatory, so gird up! God has equipped you to be a success in all He has called you to do. It would be foolish to have armor sitting around during wartime and yet never put it on. Gird yourself up in the strength of the Lord and in the power of His might. Nothing else can do this job effectively.

Fear has a way of slipping in unannounced. It often comes in the back door and just lingers about looking for an opportunity to strike. Get a little tired or sick, stretch yourself too far so that you have no time for God, watch TV or read books which feed fear and before you know it, your enemy has penetrated your camp. You are exposed and if you entertain him, like a bad guest who does not know when to leave, he will stay and invite his friends. But you can push back the enemy by meditating on God's Word. That truth will bring with it thoughts of freedom, victory, and peace. Faith will quickly defeat fear, and you will have just won another battle for your destiny.

Next, you will need to take a personal inventory. What tools has God given you? What are your gifts, your strengths, your abilities? You already know your passion, but what has He given you to accomplish that? Make a list. Include on that list people you know who may be able to help you, things you have accomplished in the past, and traits others seem to admire. Leave nothing off. This is between you and God. So be honest with yourself. He blessed you mightily, and He needs you to know that so you will use what He has given you for His purposes. This list is part of your artillery. When a soldier steps out into battle, he wants to know he is properly armed; otherwise, he will be a dead man. The same rule applies here for you.

TAKE THE STEP

"Action is a great restorer and builder of confidence. Inaction is not only the result, but the cause, of fear. Perhaps the action you take will be successful; perhaps different action or adjustments will have to follow. But any action is better than no action at all."
Norman Vincent Peale

I want you to find that heart of a champion inside of you and put your foot on the battlefield. Take the chance, take the risk and fight, you won't regret it. The great thing about fighting the giant of fear comes after you have fought your heart out. You can lie on the battlefield with the satisfaction that you took the chance. You are bruised, cut, bleeding, and tired. You are spent and have nothing else left. Yet whether or not you have won the battle, you are victorious. Again, win or lose, you still rise up the victor. You put your foot on the battlefield and you fought. You made the phone call, completed the difficult task, stood up to your opposition, disciplined your child, preached the sermon, started your own business, and declared your freedom. There is no losing in the fight. You will only lose if you never step out. That's it. And that will keep you from experiencing the most precious gift God has given you, the gift of a destiny, your destiny. So go ahead, courageously place your foot on the battlefield. This will be the fight of your life!

SECTION 4 • OVERCOMING THE PARALYSIS OF FEAR

10   E is for Establish

"May the favor of the Lord our God rest upon us; establish the work of our hands for us—yes, establish the work of our hands."
Psalm 90:17

"Every time you win, it diminishes the fear a little bit. You never really cancel the fear of losing; you keep challenging it."
Arthur Ashe

Throughout the ages, from the book of Genesis to this very day, God's people have been set apart. They are not only established in God, but they are established in the flesh. It sounds confusing, so let me explain.

In the beginning, God spoke and His verbal proclamation established the world. God established His people through His Word and by means of His grace. Before the ultimate sacrifice of Jesus Christ, God established His people through His covenants. He established kingdoms, kings, thrones, and nations. But when you leap from the Old Testament to the New something profound happens to the word establish. Its primary interpretation moves from fortifying physical kingdoms to building up the worthy Kingdom of God. But in both Testaments, establishing is accomplished inwardly first, which provides the strength needed for its outward expression.

In this chapter, we will focus on establishing your territory from those two perspectives—the inward and the outward. Only when you are aligned inwardly with God can you be established outwardly according to His will. You must understand both in order to advance further toward the fulfillment of your destiny. So buckle up for this mandatory step in overcoming the paralysis of fear. This ride promises to be bumpy!

......

Since you discovered who you are, Whose you are, and why you are here in the earlier chapters, you should now be inwardly equipped to move ahead toward your destiny. This revelation should open your eyes to the path God established for you before the beginning of time. As you progress on your journey, remember you are a mighty warrior of the Most High God put here for a purpose only you can accomplish. So let's get established.

INWARD ESTABLISHMENT

"Now He who establishes us with you in Christ and has anointed us is God, who also has sealed us and given us the Spirit in our hearts as a guarantee."
2 Corinthians 1:21-22 (NKJV)

It would be erroneous of me to assume that each person reading this has given his or her life to Christ. Nor can I assume that if you are a believer, you have completely surrendered your all to Him. But perhaps if you have gotten this far in the book, you have been moved by the message and are at least intrigued. With that said, I must make a passionate appeal. If you are one of the millions of churchgoers who considers yourself a believer because you grew up in the church and you come from a long line of believers, stop now and get things right with God. Your works will not buy salvation. Your attendance at an institution may win you badges in this world, but not in the next. God looks inward to the heart. If you love Him, repent before Him, worship and praise Him, and receive His unconditional love. Then you will walk hand in hand with the Holy Spirit—the foundation of your inward establishment.

The Holy Spirit carries with Him the battle plans for your purpose. He is that still small voice which speaks in those moments when you turn off the world and listen. His voice will direct your steps, question your decisions, and challenge your worldly thinking. His verifiable instructions without exception, line up with the Word of God. At times you will inevitably think He has left you, but He hasn't. During those moments, stop, turn down the volume around you, and be still. If you still cannot hear Him, check your heart again for things like lack of forgiveness, bitterness, and pride. These unchecked sins can cause a lot of static and make it difficult for you to hear God's message.

"So you must be patient. Establish your hearts [strengthen
and confirm them in the final certainty]."
James 5:8 (AMP)

Your heart, the second block of your inward establishment, serves as the connector between the Spirit and your faith. The heart strengthens or weakens based on your actions. If you neglect exercising your heart by expanding your knowledge of God through His Word, your faith will weaken, and fear will overtake you. You cannot hear the Holy Spirit and walk in faith without allowing God's Word to dwell within you. To establish His power within you, saturate yourself in His Word, dwell on it, meditate upon it, and seek it in all you do. Then you will recognize the voice of the Spirit and your faith will be deeply established within you too.

"But they were broken (pruned) off because of their unbelief (their lack of real faith), and you are established through faith [because you do believe]."
Romans 11:20 (AMP)

You are established through faith. Why? Is it because you are so wonderful and perfect? Is it because you are better than everyone else? Is it because you have been through more than the average person? No, no, and no! There is only one way to be established through faith and that is to believe. Belief in the Lord Jesus Christ as your Savior brings with it the Holy Spirit; belief in your heart that His Word is true strengthens your inner man. And certain belief that He is the same yesterday, today, and tomorrow establishes your faith. Feed that faith and you will be empowered for any battle life may bring your way. Stand firm in the third and final building block of your inward establishment. If you keep these three important building blocks in proper working order, you will find yourself making better decisions, being better equipped to solve life's problems, and walking in the fullness of God's grace as you live in His abundance. When you are firmly established in the Spirit, in your heart and in your faith, then everything God calls you to establish outwardly will be obvious and attainable.

THE OUTWARD ESTABLISHMENT

"...Don't be afraid of them. Remember the Lord, who is great and awesome, and fight for your brothers, your sons and your daughters, your wives and your homes."
Nehemiah 4:14

We bought our first home in Washington state sight unseen. We only knew it was located in a reputable part of town and in the center of a family friendly neighborhood. With one child and another on the way, that was important to us. It did not take long for us to discover that things were not as friendly as we were led to believe. In fact, we had moved in right next door to methamphetamine dealers! The signed contracts that made us the owners of that home did not insure the safety of our family. They did not serve to establish our freedom to enjoy the place we resided. Actually, little by little and piece by piece, we become prisoners in our own home. Then, after two years of fighting, praying, and seeking God, the phone rang. The home next door had been sold at auction. Our prayers were answered. Our hope had been restored. The fight had been won. Now we could sit back and enjoy our property. At least that is what we thought until the enemy came knocking.

The time had come for the residents of the meth house to move out. All of the neighbors watched with great anticipation, but there seemed to be no signs of an impending move. A call to the new owners revealed the unthinkable. The drug dealers had bought the home back. How could this be after we had fought so hard? We had poured ourselves out before God. We had done all we could do, or had we? Suddenly, we discovered a missed step. We had never established our fight. We made the mistake of thinking just because we had a signed deed, our job was done. But we were wrong. We had not fortified our walls, secured our territory, or taken ownership over our land. We found ourselves before God just as Nehemiah did when his enemies spoke against him in Nehemiah 4:2, *"Can they revive the stones out of the heaps of rubbish, and burned ones at that?"*

We felt like stones in the heaps of rubbish at that moment. If we did not fortify our neighborhood, the property values would plummet, the oppression would increase, and no one would be safe anymore. The enemy pressed in, and the more he pressed, the more we looked up.

At the time I didn't see the parallels our plight had with Nehemiah's plight as he sought to fortify the walls of Jerusalem. But now as I look back, I cannot help but laugh. We both received favor from those in authority to take on the challenge. We both received continual pressure from the opposition. The situation forced both of us to work with weapons (my husband painted the front of our home with a brush in his hand and a gun in his pocket). We both worked around the clock to accomplish our goals. We both struggled with discouragement throughout the process. We both became forced to work with liars, cheaters, and those who sought our destruction. But we both rose from the ashes because we trusted God over man no matter what the evidence surrounding us revealed.

It took the Jewish people fifty-two days to fortify the walls of Jerusalem. It took us thirty days to establish ours, and just as the people gathered in Jerusalem to worship and praise God, we celebrated in our cul-de-sac the day the dealers moved away. We praised God for His endless provisions and we lifted our voices to our God Most High because He acted on our behalf.

We learned many great lessons during that time in our lives. We learned to listen more to that still small voice of the Holy Spirit and to heed its direction. It became apparent that the more we listened, the louder it became. We learned that the more we poured the Word of God into our hearts, the more our faith grew. We became dependent upon Scripture in everything, thus our fear dissipated and our faith soared to new levels. And we learned that we can do all things through Christ who gives us strength. I was very sick during that time as was our daughter, and my husband worked around the clock tending to all of our needs. Obviously, in our own strength we would have failed, but in His, we emerged victorious.

Often, when stories of victory are shared, the details are left out, making others wonder what action steps brought success, so I want to share the tangible steps we took as we built up the walls around our Jerusalem and established our territory.

1. We anointed the fence posts around our home.
2. We gave our property to the Lord and declared it to be His.
3. We prayer walked our neighborhood on a regular basis.
4. We prayed for the people who came against us.
5. We prayed and asked God with expectation that He would lead us each day, and then no matter how strange the directions seemed, we did what we were told.
6. We secured a prayer team to lift us up each day.
7. We pulled the neighborhood together in the cause.
8. We praised God throughout the process.

You can apply these steps to your situation too. Whether dealing with a wayward child, a broken relationship, a struggling business, or a serious illness, these action steps will work if they are diligently applied, so use them today to establish your position after the fight.

Living through that thirty-day challenge proved an incredible experience. Now in retrospect, it seems almost surreal. In the end I became the neighborhood hero, but not because I am so great. I can guarantee you that I am not. Nor was I fearless or even courageous. I just trusted God to be who He said He was, and He heard my cries. He helped me fight the fight, and He established me inwardly and outwardly. He has faithfully established His people throughout history, and He continues to do so today.

What about you? Are you hearing that still small voice of the Holy Spirit within you? Are you neglecting Him as He tries to give you the battle plans for your destiny? Are you strengthening your heart with the Word of God so that you can hear Him better? Are you reaching for Him through His Word and prayer, or are you reaching for the telephone to get just another opinion? Are you purposefully building your faith so that when the day of adversity comes, and it will, your faith will be bigger than your fear? Or are you waiting until you need to do it? If you want to live in the fullness of God's grace for you, if you desire to live out the destiny He created for you, the time to establish yourself is now. Begin to prepare the fields for rain. Prepare your barns for the harvest. Express your faith to Him by being ready in and out of season.

You are special to God. He wants to be in fellowship with you. He longs to lead you just as He has led and established David, Noah, Job, Jonah, Abraham, Nehemiah, and countless others. He is no respecter of persons. If He planned a purpose for you than He is prepared to help you see it through. And if He is giving you air in your lungs, then your destiny is not complete.

You have fought, you have established, and in the process you have learned many lessons. Post guards around your new territory. Polish your armor. Grab your sword, and saddle up. Now it is time to advance!

SECTION 4 • OVERCOMING THE PARALYSIS OF FEAR

11   A is for Advance

"With your help I can advance against a troop,
with my God I can scale a wall."
2 Samuel 22:30

"If one advances confidently in the direction of his dreams,
and endeavors to live the life which he has imagined,
he will meet with a success unexpected in common hours."
Henry David Thoreau

You have established your fight, you have fortified your camp, and you have secured your territory. Now, you are positioned to advance confidently and with more faith than fear!

You may still feel fear on some level, but you've laid the ground work so that your larger faith defeats your fear. You have walked through an experience that has proven you can indeed do all things through Christ who gives you strength. The key point as you advance further is to know that God is with you. He is the supplier of your strength. You may believe in God, but if you do not know He is with you, you will still lack the confidence you need for victory. The fact that you survived the fight and are here to tell about it should serve as a reminder that God was with you, and He still is today. He is glorified when His children live out their destinies. Remember that as the desire to settle begins to come over you.

Abraham's father understood the desire to settle. The Bible doesn't tell us much about Terah, but one profound sentence in Genesis 11:31 reveals volumes. Terah and his family set out for the land of Canaan (The Promised Land). His decision to better the lives of his family never reached fulfillment. At the end of verse 31, we read, *"BUT when they came to Haran, they SETTLED there"* (emphasis mine). Terah died where he settled, and so will you. It may not be today or even tomorrow, but when you settle, you stop living with purpose. This is not to say that you should move around, or that you should not be content. The kind of settling I am talking about is completely different. God ordered Terah to move his family to Canaan, yet he stopped short and settled for less than what God had for him.

We settle when we stop believing there is more to do. We settle when we think we have done enough. We settle when we stop trusting and when we fear adversity will come. This mindset will not only keep you from advancing, but it will put you back into fear. Then the ground you gained in the fight and that you established in the aftermath will be lost once again.

Abraham learned from his father, and serves as one of the greatest examples of one who advanced through life with God. Abraham had no visions of grandeur about the life he would live. He did not have a list of goals he wanted to accomplish in his lifetime. As a matter of fact, when God came to him in Chapter 12 of Genesis and told him to leave his country and go to the land God would show him, Abraham was seventy-five years old. He could easily have settled and anyone would have understood if he did, but Abraham listened to God, packed up his family, and walked wherever the Lord led him. God gave him no written instructions, deed, or title. What He did give him though was a promise:

"I will make you into a great nation and I will bless you.
I will make your name great, and you will be a blessing.
I will bless those who bless you, and whoever curses you I will curse;
and all peoples on earth will be blessed through you."
Genesis 12:2-3

I love the next line, *"So Abram left..."* (Genesis 12:4). He didn't demand all of the steps. He didn't question God about the future. He just left. Is there any doubt in your mind as to why this man is known as the Father of Faith? God said go. God told him why. And he went. So simple, yet...

Are you one of those who need to know what steps two, three, four, and five are before you take step one? Do you need to fully understand everything before you do anything? Do you need to do everything perfectly or not at all? If you answered yes to any or all of these questions, then you will be stuck in Haran instead of moving on to your Promised Land. Let me help you move. First, God does not promise to give you every step; otherwise, you will be less likely to move. Second, you will never fully understand everything. It is impossible, so stop trying. And lastly, you are not perfect and you never will be. But guess what? Nobody else is perfect either, so stop expecting them to be! I can speak so candidly because I have been there myself, and it caused me to settle. I am grateful for the mentors in my life who gave it to me straight. The sooner you conquer that giant, the sooner you will get your bags packed and head out for the land of the living!

"Courage is fear that has said its prayers and
decided to go forward anyway."
Joyce Meyer

My favorite definition of the word advance, from the Merriam -Webster Dictionary, is "to move ahead toward a goal." To move ahead, to take action, to get requires something from us. God has the ability to give His children anything, but when it comes to our destinies, He requires us to take action and to move ahead toward His goal for us. Working for what you have builds great character. Parents discovered this generations ago. You do your children a great disservice if you never let them earn anything. God knows that better than anyone. The more He did for the Israelites, the more they complained. And therefore God did not allow them to advance physically until they had advanced spiritually.

Heroes inhabit the battlefields of life. Character comes from those moments of testing when the world has lost its belief in you. James explains those incredible times of testing so well in James 1:2-4, *"Consider it pure joy, my brothers, whenever you face trials of many kinds, because you know that the testing of your faith develops perseverance. Perseverance must finish its work so that you may be mature and complete, not lacking anything."*

Many times, as you advance toward your destiny, you will need to persevere. The sun may not be shining, the economy may have hit rock bottom, your friends and family may not be for you, your hopes for the future may seem bleak, but you will need to find the warrior inside of you and step out. Gird yourself up for battle and march into the enemy territory.

"When David was told of this, he gathered all Israel and crossed the Jordan; he advanced against them and formed his battle lines opposite them."
I Chronicles 19:17

Before entering battle, check for enemies within your camp. You know how to recognize fear, but one quirky foe sneaks in easily and unnoticed. This one tells you that you are just not in the right mood to do it today. Your hormones are out of control, the kids are sick, the house payment is late, you didn't get enough sleep last night, somebody is mad at you, you'll never meet the deadline anyway so why bother, or you just don't FEEL like it. That's right; the quirky foe I speak of is your feelings.

Your feelings will kill your destiny. If you have mustered up the strength to fight your giant and establish your territory, your feelings now will convince you of all the reasons why you need a break. Now your feelings will want you to settle. After all, getting here was so hard, why keep going? You have accomplished this much. Isn't that good enough? Your feelings will keep you from advancing, and if you allow yourself to be entertained by them, they will ultimately lead you back to fear. Feelings and fear can be allies against you, so beware of this trap.

"In his heart a man plans his course, but the
LORD determines his steps."
Proverbs 16:9

There is not one set way to advance your territory. The actual steps will be different for each person depending on your calling. The common denominator between all advancing warriors is the need to persist. You cannot go out to advance with an attitude of "I'll give it a shot, but if it doesn't work, I'll give it up." No! Advancing, like fighting, must have your full commitment from start to finish, and you must be flexible with God about the date of completion. That does not mean you cannot have a goal date, by all means do, but be prepared to allow God to lead the charge, and trust that He knows what is best.

When I began writing this book, I had no idea what it was going to take to complete it. If I had known what was going to be required of me, I would have been tempted to run in the other direction. But instead, I moved forward. I set goals and God changed them. I made plans and God adjusted them. I learned throughout the process to live like David, Joshua, Moses, Abraham, and Esther and just trust God with my future. You too will have a higher success rate if you will trust Him with His plans for you.

Successful people who continue to be successful have one thing in common: they continue to advance in their field. Whether we are talking about large corporations like Apple which stays on the cutting edge of technology or athletes like quarterback Kurt Warner who continued to train and develop his skills throughout his career. Advancing is a must. Many successful businesses suffer the fatal blow when they stop growing. They refuse to grow with new technology. They refuse to expand and take risks, so another similar business willing to be set apart comes along and advances. Soon the advancing business dominates the market and the complacent one dies. A competitor is waiting to take your position. If you establish without advancing, you relinquish your future territory to them.

I understand the resistance to advancing all too well. My husband and I are what many would call right-brained, artistic, free-flowing people. For this reason we have always been self-employed. We spent years convincing ourselves that God made us this way, and we did not need to evolve with current technology. What a lie that we swallowed. Little by little, the truth revealed that if we wanted to go where God wanted to take us, we needed to catch up with technology. This was not a fun time for us. We still find new technology uncomfortable, but we did it. We chose to advance in this area so that we could truly walk out the destiny we were called to live.

"What saves a man is to take a step. Then another step."
C. S. Lewis

For years, I spent a lot of money on myself, but not in the ways you may think. I wasn't spending money on spas, manicures, or facials (maybe a pedicure every now and then). But I did spend money on advancing myself. I am a great investment, and so are you. Because of that, I spend money on books, CDs, manuals, trainings, Bibles, worship music, and coaching. I will invest in anything that will develop me as a person. I will invest in education so that I can be excellent at what I put my hands to. I consider this investment far more valuable than nice homes and expensive cars. This money actually advances me forward, and every step I take forward puts me that much closer to my destiny.

Whether you are a pastor, a business owner, a network marketer, a college student, a stay-at-home mom, an executive, or an employee, make the commitment to invest in yourself. Making that crucial investment will change your life if you follow through and apply the lessons you learn. Go to events that will help you in your field, listen to teleseminars, watch webinars, read books, take classes, get coaching, or find a trainer. Whether you are advancing your career, taking control of your health, getting in shape, or becoming a better parent, get the help you need to be your best.

The problem with living in a fast food society with our microwave mentality is that people want things now. They want to be famous, successful, or even notorious, and they want it now. That is why people fall into get rich quick schemes and take ridiculous risks in the market.

But the true success which comes from overcoming the paralysis of fear and stepping into your destiny does not happen overnight. David didn't have time to think about taking down that giant, but he had prepared himself for such a moment. I am sure in his wildest imagination he never dreamed he would be taking on a giant and killing him with a slingshot. But he prepared himself for whatever God had for him by doing his best at every challenge God gave him. He developed the skill of using the sling shot because he worked diligently at tending his father's sheep. He didn't just run from the lions and bears and apologize to his father for losing another of the flock. No, he wanted to honor his father. That is why he felt prepared to step into his destiny. His preparation helped to relieve him of the fear I am sure he felt as he approached the giant that fateful day. Because of that, he advanced, and he spent the rest of his life advancing.

I prepared myself for years to be doing what I do today, although I had no idea at the time. I can remember always loving the stage. The years I spent singing, playing instruments, and acting helped prepare me for the life I now live. As a child, I sang into my hairbrush in front of the mirror. I took voice lessons and sang in the choir. In August of 2008, I realized a lifelong dream when I sang in front of thousands of people. I had prepared my whole life for that moment, so when it arrived, I was ready.

While reading an old journal one day, I found an interesting entry. Several years ago, I wrote, "I have been working on a motivational speech entitled 'Who Am I.' I believe I am being led into a leadership role and will be speaking to large groups, so I am preparing." Two years later I taught that lesson for the first time to a group of over five hundred women, but I practiced it for two years in the car, in my office, in the shower, and in even in my sleep! I prepared for advancement, and so should you.

How do troops prepare to advance further? They train people. They make sure they have the necessary supplies. They scope out the territory. They know their destination and what conditions they may find. They work hard to eliminate any surprises. And even after all of that, they prepare for the worst. Although not expecting the worst, they are still prepared for it. That is wisdom. Now, please do not be a glass half empty person and always expect the worst. Instead, diligently prepare by acquiring knowledge that will help you eradicate the fear that would otherwise derail you. Be ready to confront any situation. Prepare for rain and keep your umbrella handy.

"The bottom line in leadership isn't how far we advance ourselves;
it is how far we advance others."
John Maxwell

One of the most important steps in advancing is mentoring. When you pour out to others your hard-earned life lessons, you help them advance further along on the battlefield. People love to hear stories of victory because it gives them hope. It builds their courage. When God pours into you, you have the responsibility to then pour into others. If God pours into you, you become full. If you do not pour out, there will be no reason for Him to keep filling you. And who wouldn't want fresh infillings from the Lord? It is simple, I know, but it goes along with one of my favorite Bible verses, *"Give and it will be given to you. A good measure, pressed down, shaken together and running over, will it be poured into your lap"* (Luke 6:38). When you teach and mentor others, you also cement in your mind what you have learned. I have been known to call people and preach a sermon to them about what I just learned from my Bible study. That way, I advance my learning and they learn something new too. It is a win-win. Both of us are moved that much further out. Teaching and mentoring others will help push you beyond your established battlefield and advance you further.

Don't make the mistake of getting caught up in your comfort zone. Your comfort zone will always be anywhere other than the battlefield. It will always be set back away from the action. And you want to be where the action is because where there is action, there is victory; where there is victory, there is life. You don't have to succeed every time to find His joy and peace in the midst of the battle. You just need to know that you are walking your anointed calling. So if you feel called to sing, then sing. If you feel called to write a book, then write it. If you feel called to preach, then preach the truth. Know your calling to teach and don't hide your light under a bushel or bury your talents. God gave you abilities to be used, not hidden. Whether you are a stay-at-home mother, a banker, a realtor, a network marketer, a tradesman, an assistant, a CEO, a student, a teacher, or a door-to-door salesperson, you were called to do your best, to be your best, and to glorify God in the process. And as you walk in your calling remember, *"Whatever you do, do it heartily as unto the Lord and not to man"* (Colossians 3:23). When you do that, you will advance. Walking in excellence will be your assurance.

Reach out. Stretch yourself. Be willing to grow. Go out there and enlarge your territory! This is what advancement is all about. Move ahead, so that you will not fall behind.

So how do you advance?

1. Get the training, coaching, and mentoring you need.

2. Read, study, and grow in your calling.
3. Set new goals.
4. Stretch yourself.
5. Dream bigger.
6. Mentor others.
7. Enlarge your territory.
8. Seek God in all things.

You have fought. You have established. And you have advanced. Now that you have succeeded in furthering the Kingdom of God and are marching forward with a warrior's determination to accomplish His purpose for you, you have made yourself a more visible target for your enemy. He has put a contract out on you, BUT never fear, you have been armed with all of the knowledge, wisdom and understanding you need to thwart his attacks. He will come at you with everything. Now, prepare to resist.

SECTION 4 • OVERCOMING THE PARALYSIS OF FEAR

12   R is for Resist

"Be self-controlled and alert. Your enemy the Devil prowls around like a roaring lion looking for someone to devour. Resist him, standing firm in the faith."
2 Peter 5:8-9

"We gain the strength of the temptation we resist."
Ralph Waldo Emerson

If you are one of those people who prefer to use only happy, positive words, you may not like the word resist. I happen to think it is a very positive word because of the results it produces. You have just fought your heart out. You have worked to keep the ground you gained by establishing yourself. You even stepped out to take more ground by advancing. Why would you not want to resist losing it all? Resisting after receiving is a good thing. Let me show you why.

To resist means to stand, to oppose, or to fend off. My favorite definition is to hold one's ground. To hold one's ground! Think about that. Just as a child refuses to let go of the toy they finally got their hands on, you need to express that same tenacity. You have gained valuable ground. The person you have become in the process is priceless, so why would you not want to hold your ground?

I am going to discuss in depth several key areas where you will need to resist if you want to rise up victorious. Some of them may hit a little close to home. Others may not be a problem for you. But all of them have been culprits in keeping warriors in bondage to fear, so they need to be eradicated.

First of all, you will need to...

RESIST TOXIC PEOPLE

"Look out for the good things, not the faults. It takes a good deal bigger-sized brain to find out what is not wrong with people and things than to find out what is wrong."
R.L. Sharpe

We are talking about resisting things that may draw you back into negativity and fear, like toxic people. I am a fan of nutritional cleansing (www.wantmorehealth.com). I believe we are bombarded with toxins on a daily basis and our bodies need constant help with eliminating them. If you do not remove the toxins, your body will become over-burdened and the result will be sickness and disease. The same is true with toxic people. Hanging out with toxic people will make you sick; it will make you broken, it will make you negative, and it will make you doubt yourself. If you are not resisting toxic people, you could be jeopardizing the victory you have gained.

Toxic people are constantly negative. They don't see the bright side of anything. They question everything you do which keeps you in a constant state of doubt. They expect you to quit or fail. They are victims in their own lives. Guard yourself from these people. You may not be able to completely eliminate them in your life, but you can protect yourself from them still. When you do see them or talk to them, try to keep the subject on them and keep it short. These people are emotional vampires, so wear a turtleneck for protection! Just an aside, these types of people do need to be ministered to, but just make sure you are pouring into their lives without allowing them to drain you in the process.

If toxic people make up most of your social contact list, make an effort to find positive, like-minded people who are warriors too. Find people who will build you up and not tear you down. They are out there. When you find them, make sure you are not a toxic person to them! Flee from your old ways. Learn to be one who encourages and builds up. You will get what you give in this life, so give good stuff away.

Next…

RESIST THE TEMPTATION TO RETURN TO YOUR OLD FEARFUL SELF

*"In God's economy, a person must go down into the valley of grief
before he or she can scale the heights of spiritual glory…
One must come to the end of 'self' before
one can really begin to live."*
Billy Graham

As you maintain your position of victory, you will need to resist the temptation to return to your old, fearful, immovable self. Resist that person who was too fearful to make the phone calls. Resist the one who was afraid to approach successful business people. Resist the temptation to return to the person who was afraid to start a new business, afraid to defend yourself, afraid to stand up for your principles, afraid to start over after divorce or financial setback, afraid to say no to your kids, or afraid to take control of your health. Flee from the temptation to go back to being walked on or trampled over. When you have done all else, stand. Stand firm and resist.

Know that when you choose to enter the battlefield, you will experience attacks. When you step out into your greatness, you will be confronted. Resist the attacks. Know the source of your hope. The enemy comes to steal, kill, and destroy, but you are a mighty warrior of the Most High God. You have made it this far. Put up your shield of faith and resist those attacks. When the lie that you are not good enough comes up, remind yourself who you are in Christ. When the temptation to compare yourself with others begins to plague you, remember how God has chosen the most unlikely to carry out His work. Remember when the fear of man begins to make you doubt what you are doing that you perform for an audience of One. Remember in those moments, you have the power to declare that no weapon formed against you will prosper. Use your artillery and your authority. You have been freed from the miry pit of fear; resist the temptation to go back.

Then…

RESIST DISTRACTIONS
HOW DISTRACTION LEADS TO DESTRUCTION

"There has to be a definite purpose and goal if you are to progress. If you are not intent about what you are doing, you aren't able to resist the temptation to do something else that might be more fun at the moment."
John Wooden

Distractions surround us and constantly lure us away from our destinies. Some distractions are good things, but you will need to learn how and when to keep them at bay. For those of you who have home-based businesses, this is a big one. Endless distractions require a lot of resistance if we are to make it to the finish line.

My husband and I both work from home and we home school our children. This means that nearly every day, people fill our home, and we all have things to accomplish. When I am in the throes of doing something which I either do not like to do or that intimidates me, I can be easily distracted. That is when my commitment comes in, and I must force myself to stick with the plan. I have often written agreements with myself and even with my family, so that I will have something to remind me why I need to stay on track.

Distractions come in many different forms. Most American families have one huge distraction in common—a large rectangular box which sits in most living rooms, media rooms, bedrooms, kitchens, and family rooms across the country. I think of the TV as the escape hatch. This magical box will transform the world around you as it takes you off to some other place far, far away from your problems. With this distraction, you live vicariously through other people. You rejoice with them when they win and hurt with them when they lose, but you do it all without any risk or pain of your own. And although the getaway is nice at times, too many holidays with this mystical box will keep you from accomplishing great things in your lifetime. You will not face your fears and take on giants by watching other people do it. You need to get out and take the action yourself. And although you can be motivated by the stories of other people, if they only serve to entertain you and not to move you into action, they are just another distraction. And distractions lead to the destruction of destinies.

TV is addicting. I know this because I had to give mine away once. I could not control myself with it. Now, I have a media room with a large TV with surround sound which I use to watch Joyce Meyer or *Life Today* while I work out, and I enjoy episodes of *Little House on the Prairie* or *The Waltons* with my family on Sunday night. Other than that, it is a box which takes up space. Control in this area is essential. When you want to tune out, be aware of what you are tuning into.

Other common distractions can be reading fiction, shopping, eating out, obsessive working out (unless your goal is to be an Olympic champion or a professional athlete), hanging out with friends, watching movies, and spending too much time on the computer. The list goes on, but you get the point. Now, do not misunderstand me here. I do not want you to think you should never have fun and just relax. I like to have fun and hang out with friends. I like to read a good book occasionally that has nothing to do with my destiny. I also enjoy having a nice meal out and shopping. What we fail to do sometimes, though, is to remember the word occasionally. Everything in moderation leads to a healthy and balanced life. Many of us escape the responsibility of living up to our destiny by being easily distracted. As if it were not hard enough twenty years ago, now we have the computer, cell phones, Twitter, Facebook, texting and whatever new technology is being invented while I write this.

It requires discipline to avoid distractions. Sometimes we need to remove ourselves completely from areas of distraction so that we can resist them. Whatever it takes, do it. Resisting will become easier; especially as you begin to see the success you seek. Focus your time on feeding your mind. This is hard at first, but if overcoming the paralysis of fear is important to you, you will make the necessary changes.

When you do this, don't forget to.....

RESIST THE TEMPTATION TO MAKE EXCUSES

"He that is good for making excuses is seldom good for anything else."
Benjamin Franklin

A corporate trainer friend of mine uses a silly little phrase to drive home a great point. If you try to give him an excuse of any kind, he'll look you in the eyes and say, "I'm all out of peanut butter." The lesson in this ridiculous statement is that any excuse you can come up with sounds just as silly. Excuses only serve to belittle the greatness of God. Sure, in your own strength you probably cannot do what you dream of doing and that is just the way God wants it. In Judges 7:2, God tells Gideon, *"You have too many men for me to deliver Midian into their hands. In order that Israel may not boast against me that her own strength saved her..."* God wanted Gideon to be in the position to be unable to accomplish the task alone. Then when God moved, He would be glorified and Gideon could take no credit. That is where He wants you too. He does not want to hear why you can't, but rather why He can.

As a life and leadership coach, I have heard just about every excuse in the book. As a human being, I have given just about every excuse in the book, and I created a few new ones in the process. As a mother, I have made it a point not to allow my kids to short change themselves by making excuses. Excuses only serve to extinguish the fire of God within you. They cheapen not just the gifts of God but your intrinsic value as well.

When I was sick, I lost my temper a lot. It is funny what happens to your mind when you are not getting adequate nutrition. My behavior horrified me, since before the sickness I had a pretty calm demeanor, although I could be a hyper person. Day in and day out, God broke me when I lost my temper, acted like a baby, humiliated myself in front of my son, and ran off to my room crying. Through it all, God never allowed me the freedom to make excuses. So I repented, took my son in my arms, asked for his forgiveness, and told him that Mommy got a God swat. By explaining to him that there is never an excuse for sin, not even sickness, I taught him not to be an excuse maker. So I tell you now, take your God swats and stop making excuses. God created you for a reason. Find that reason and then find reasons why you can instead of reasons why you can't. Don't diminish the capacity of your infinite God by making excuses for your finite self.

RESISTANCE TRAINING

The small nagging fears like talking to people, receiving rejection, or simply failing more often keep us from our destinies than the overbearing fears such as sky diving, flying, or scuba diving. But interestingly enough, small fears taken in small bites are not all that hard to overcome. Yet they keep us paralyzed. This is where resistance training comes in handy.

Resistance trainers know that starting a program with weights that are too heavy spells failure. You not only risk injury, but you more likely will lose hope in your lifting abilities. Any good trainer will start a new, inexperienced person with less weight and more repetitions. The more you build up in your workout, the more confidence you have. The more confidence you have, the more weight you are will attempt. It is amazing not only to watch, but even more so to experience.

When I started using a personal trainer, the things I was able to do as I built up my strength amazed me. I gained confidence to do more and more. I have seen this happen time and time again as I have coached people. Those scared to death to speak in front of large audiences transform into mic hogs. Just like you and me, they had their own set of baggage to sort through, and they did it piece by piece. They started by remaining seated and sharing a word or two in a room of people. Then they shared a statement. Next, they moved to the front of the room to give a testimony. And finally, they moved confidently onto the stage and inspired the masses with their ability to overcome!

You use the same technique to overcome the paralysis of fear. If phone calls scare you, don't decide to make fifty calls one day just to prove you can do it. Start with one. I can guarantee one thing. If you make that call and you have success with it, you will voluntarily pick up the phone to make another one. But if the one call does not go well and you put on your list to make fifty calls, misery and lack of energy will come across in your voice. So make the one call. Then each day, add another call until you get to the desired amount. You can apply this principle to anything that requires action.

If you fear talking to strangers, start with small steps like smiling. Once you see that many people actually smile back, you will feel like you can venture out and say hello. Keep stretching yourself until you get to the point that you can have a conversation with them. The most important thing to remember is that everyone has a favorite subject, and it tends to be them. By asking about them, you do not even need to be a great conversationalist, but they will think you are. Learn the power of asking questions and you will not only be a hit at any party, but you will also be on your way to overcoming the paralysis of fear. Become an expert in resistance training.

MY CHAMPION
HOW SMALL PEOPLE CAN TAKE ON BIG GIANTS

Some people are forced to come into this world as fighters like my sister, Beth. Beth was born in 1966 with a cleft lip and pallet. She spent her life in and out of hospitals as the doctors tried to repair the damage. In spite of it all, Beth had an incredible propensity to love and she possessed the heart of a champion.

From an early age, Beth knew that she wanted to be a nurse. Because of the love she had been shown by nurses as a child, she wanted to be there to help scared little girls and boys as they fought to overcome the health challenges they had been born with.

Beth fought her whole life. I do not remember a time that anything came easy to her, except when she loved. That was second nature to her. Beth fought for every good grade she collected, and she fought to be on honor roll. She fought to learn to play clarinet even with the deformities in her mouth, lip, and nose. She fought to learn piano and to try to stay one step ahead of her younger sister (I fought not to let that happen!). She fought to keep the peace in our family which often meant she had to fight for her life as she placed herself dangerously between her two sisters.

I will never forget the year Beth was able to compete for the local Miss Teen pageant. This was a big achievement for her because Beth lacked confidence in her appearance, and she certainly felt discomfort in front of large groups of people. The memory of her coming out on stage and performing a flag routine to "Uptown Girl" by Billy Joel is a moment etched in my mind forever. There was never a time I was more proud of her. Beth placed 2nd in that competition. And that accomplishment put another fight under her belt.

Beth continued to fight, establish, and advance as she took on the countless giants that surrounded her. She saw so much victory, because in the midst of it all, she never stopped resisting the urge to quit. And trust me, she wanted to quit. She could have quit too. Everyone would have understood and no one would have faulted her because of the many challenges she faced. But always determined to overcome, this small-framed, petite girl grew into a woman with a big dream and an uncompromising belief that she would accomplish her goal, and that was to obtain her degree in nursing.

I have never witnessed more resistance than I did as Beth struggled through nursing school. Every time she came home, my mother and I needed to convince her to go back. She usually cried and refused, but by the time Sunday afternoon rolled around, she always stick her chin up, swung her head around, and drove back to school to take on her giant one more week.

Beth passed her nursing exam. She found a great job at a reputable hospital, but Beth decided to continue striving for excellence. She attended a local school and worked while she obtained her bachelor degree in nursing. As if this were still not enough, she took on another giant and headed back to school for her master's degree. I would love to say she accomplished this goal, but on December 22, 1992, Beth fought her last fight. This champion, my champion, went to be with Jesus after being killed in a car accident. The victory was still hers though. She had fought the desire to rebel against God and had won. She had established herself as a Christian in her life. She had advanced the kingdom by sharing her faith with others. And she had resisted the temptation to turn away from the God she loved and served.

How could someone so small take on such big giants? She never let fear determine her future. Beth became a champion because no matter how bad her circumstances looked, she saw only her outcome, and she learned early that champions become champions by resisting the desire to return to normal.

RESIST THE DEVIL

How could I possibly write a chapter on resisting without stating the obvious? The destructive fear that wants to keep you from fulfilling your destiny is not from God. It is a trick and a tool used by the evil one to keep you from the fullness of God. But you have power over him. How do I know this? James told us in James 4:7-8 when he wrote, *"Submit yourselves, then, to God. Resist the Devil, and he will flee from you. Come near to God and he will come near to you."*

Submission to God gives you the power to resist the Devil. Rest assured that being near to God (seeking Him in His Word, praying continually to Him, serving Him, and loving His people) will give you the supernatural ability to resist the Devil and cause him to flee. The name of Jesus contains infinite power! Praise be to God!

RESISTANCE EXERCISES

What about you? Are you ready to resist the temptation to return to your old ways? Take the time to answer the questions below. The answers are between you and God, so be honest with yourself. The only person you hurt by denying the truth is you. This is about your destiny.

This is about your future. The future God prepared for you before the beginning of time, so take it seriously. This is not about beating yourself up. You have done that enough already. This is simply about facing the truth so that you can move ahead and have the life of your dreams.

QUESTIONS TO PONDER

Who are the toxic people in your life?

_____

_____

If you have many of them, ask yourself why?

_____

_____

Is there something in the way you act that is attracting negative people?

_____

_____

If you answered yes, find help to overcome that. There are great books, CDs, coaches, sermons, and Scriptures to help you. (I am a fan of Joyce Meyer, Dani Johnson, Lance Wallnau, and Beth Moore when it comes to personal development and highly recommend you use their resources).

Learn Scripture to aid you in attack. List 5 here.

_____

_____

_____

_____

_____

What are some things that have been distracting you?

_____

_____

What changes will you make today that would help propel you toward your destiny?

_____

_____

_____

_____

What excuses for failure have you been making?

_____

_____

_____

_____

At first, resisting seems like a lot of work. You may find yourself feeling deprived and separated from all of the fun. But if you resist the temptation to allow yourself to entertain those thoughts, you will experience greater victory than you ever imagined, and you will wonder why you ever wasted so much time on such silly things.

You are being set free! Your chains are breaking. Your prison door is opening, and on the other side your destiny awaits. Will you step out? Will you trust God? Will you take the risk and resist the desire to stay comfortable? Only you can write the end of this story. This book has been about your destiny and your purpose. What will you do with the knowledge?

DEFEATING FEAR

CONCLUSION

"O LORD, truly I am your servant; I am your servant, the son of your maidservant; you have freed me from my chains."
Psalm 116:16

"When you face your fear, most of the time you will discover that it was not really such a big threat after all. We all need some form of deeply rooted, powerful motivation / it empowers us to overcome obstacles so we can live our dreams."
Les Brown
American author, entrepreneur, & motivational speaker

Now that you've learned some proven ways to overcome the paralysis of fear plus the key steps to victory, you have two options. You can put the principles you have been taught into action, or you can put this book down, check it off as read, and go onto the next one, doing nothing. It is not enough to read books, listen to audio recordings, or go to seminars and church services. To truly learn and benefit from these resources, you must implement the lessons you have learned. The best way to solidify your victory over the paralysis of fear is by teaching others. When you teach others, you are speaking out of your mouth the meditations of your heart. You are reaching into the recesses of your mind and retrieving the data that would otherwise be lost. By using these principles, you will gain the confidence necessary to stop the paralysis of fear. You will sharpen your intuition so that when the lies of fear wrap their tentacles around your dreams, your awareness of the attack will enable you to fight, establish, advance, and resist!

The life that you want will come from the habits you develop. Practice the habits that produce the life you want. Habits are formed by making decisions and sticking to them. Overcoming the paralysis of fear is a decision. It is a simple act of surrender. It is a step that will yield a great harvest like you have never known before. But there will be no growth without surrender. Remember you must give something up in order to get something better. Can you think of anything better to give up than fear itself? I once heard a pastor say that for an acorn to become an oak, it must give up the right to ever be an acorn again. Today, you are that acorn. You have the right to stay just where you are, safe and warm in your little crusty shell. You also have the opportunity to surrender yourself, to break free from the bondage you call security, so you can bloom and grow. An acorn does not become a mighty oak overnight and neither will you become a mighty warrior overnight. However, with patience, resilience, faith, hope, trust, and total reliance on the Holy Spirit who meets you in your weakness and helps you overtake your obstacles, you, like the mighty oak, will conquer stagnation. You will push past pain, overcome the damage from exterior forces, and continue to grow mightier. Until finally you will tower over the darkness of desperation, wave your arms in the air with total abandon, and live a life of freedom and victory. Choose this day to surrender to the Lord Most High—your destiny is waiting!

"Now may the God of peace [Who is the Author and the Giver of peace], Who brought again from among the dead our Lord Jesus, that great Shep-

herd of the sheep, by the blood [that sealed, ratified] the everlasting
agreement (covenant, testament), Strengthen (complete, perfect) and
make you what you ought to be and equip you with everything good that
you may carry out His will; [while He Himself] works in you and
accomplishes that which is pleasing in His sight, through
Jesus Christ (the Messiah); to Whom be the glory
forever and ever (to the ages of the ages). Amen (so be it)."
Hebrews 13:20-21 (AMP)

DEFEATING FEAR

AFTERWORD

God birthed this book through me while I was in the midst of the battle with the fear many American families face today—the fear of foreclosure. This oppressive fear differs from many of the other destiny destroying fears in that it is so personal and it carries with it the all consuming fear of failure. Although I am still facing the aftermath of the foreclosure process, I am here to tell you I did survive and I did so by applying the steps you just learned from the pages of this book.

One month after we left our home, I shared my story with the world on my website at www.CarrieCStone.com. I was reluctant to do so out of fear that I would be judged and ridiculed, or that I would destroy my ministry before it even began. I shared the story on Facebook with the caption "If God were not glorified in this, I would be horrified." Truer words were never written. I could not believe the response I received from people all over the world. Because of that, I thought it would be fitting to share that blog post with you as we end our time here together.

I pray that by sharing my experience with you, you will find hope in your current situation, and you will stand up in courage, step onto the battlefield and fight for your destiny.

IF MY HOUSE COULD TALK

Recently, my husband and I experienced something most wish never to face, but far too many in our society are encountering today. We, like millions of other hard working, big dreaming Americans have lost our home to foreclosure due to the real estate collapse. This is probably one of the hardest things we have ever had to experience. Not so much because of the loss of the house and our retirement, but because of the loss of relationship from some we thought would never desert us, and because of my passion for integrity which I have taught for twenty-two years. Hard work made no difference. Planning and ingenuity failed us. But God in His righteousness and goodness came through for us in a mighty way. Because of His care, we were able to move into a beautiful home RENT free for as many years as we need to recover. And we were able to do that two months prior to the auction of our home.

I posted a comment on Facebook the day after my final visit to our beautiful home which my husband so lovingly built with his own two hands. I was trying to be funny in my comment, maybe just to ease the pain by saying, "I went to say one last good-bye to my house yesterday. It had no response!" But the outpouring of love I received brought me to tears and to this page to share my thoughts with you. One special woman wrote the following message: "A real loss. Grieve it. Ask: What would my house have said back to me as I said good-bye?" These words caused me to cry. Even now as I read them again, I cannot help but to be broken before God as to wipe the tears from my eyes. You see, although God provided for us in a mighty way and we are beyond grateful for His grace toward us, we still have feelings, emotions, and pain. We can't ignore the feelings of loss and yes, even failure. Dealing with that is important. So I will heed the wise advice of my dear friend and post the following:

"If My House Could Talk."

If my house could talk, what would it say? First I think it would say, "Thank you." "Thank you, Rod, for pouring your heart out for me. You did a fine job with excellent craftsmanship. There is not one area where you did not go above and beyond what was needed or expected. What I appreciated the most about you was that you didn't curse even when you were tired, and you were patient with everyone who worked for you even in the midst of stress and exhaustion. Thank you, Carrie, for insisting there be Scriptures put into my foundation and then into my walls. That made me stronger and will carry me a long way in this world where buildings grow tired and weary and finally break down. Thanks to all of you for the love, laughter, singing, and worship which flowed through my halls and up to my rafters. I have always carried a spirit of peace because of that. Thank you for meeting every morning in my prayer window as you discussed the world events, the Word of God, and the future together. The strength in your relationship will be felt in this dwelling for its life. Thank you for tending to my dings and scratches and for protecting me from the destruction of children. I always appreciated it when I heard you scold Newell and Olivia, Carrie, by saying, "You may not treat our home that way. Do you not remember how very hard your father worked to build this for us?" I always felt safe with the two of you. Thank you for being silly, for taking time to dance around on my hardwood floors, for anointing every window and doorway, for falling on your knees and often on your face as you worked with all of your heart and prayed with all of your spirit to keep me as part of your family. Your tears will forever be a part of me. I heard you as you cried out to God, and I wept with you. On those late nights, as you paced the floor searching for answers, I was up with you. And even though I know you are already aware of this, God was here every second of every day. When you cried, He cried too. When you worshiped in spite of the circumstances, He smiled. And the day you finally threw up your hands and surrendered, He was the one who caught you as collapsed and grieved over your loss.

"The love your family left is overwhelming. You are all so close that it will not matter where you live, your love will be your greatest treasure. I admit I will not miss the pink bunny, but I will miss the two little people who created his life. Even though I cannot go with you, the memories you created here will be yours forever. Remember what Olivia said about needing to come back to get her memories? Well, she already had them with her. I think she discovered that when she saw my empty shell. You packed everything that matters in this life. Treasure that. Treasure the worship nights in the living room, the Sorry games at the kitchen table, the family devotion times, the jokes told, the meals prepared together, the Christmas you were snowed in, the nights on the deck, the mornings of snuggles, the school days in the school room, the book written, the songs created and recorded, the celebration as Rod's song "USA Today" was performed on live TV by Lee Greenwood, the family get-togethers, the long nights of Scrabble, and the baths in the big tub. The bank cannot take those. They are yours to keep, so cherish them.

"One day, you will think of me and it will not hurt. Instead, you will remember the good times. Until then, know that in every crevice, in every corner, in every tiny bit of this home, your family can be found. You have made me unique. You have made me special. And the next family who lives here will be blessed by what you have left behind."

Thank you for indulging me today by allowing me to express my heart to you. Maybe you have something or someone you need to say good-bye to. Take the time to do that today. It may hurt for a moment, but it will release you to live out God's purposes for you. Do it today! Your destiny is waiting!

CONNECT WITH

CARRIE

f
www.facebook.com/carriecstone

www.twitter.com/carriecstone

www.carriecstone.com

e
carrie@carriecstone.com

Nothing would thrill me more than to hear from you! I have a passion for seeing God's people live out their destinies. I am excited about the opportunity to connect with you as you boldly take on your giants and fulfill God's purposes for you. Please feel free to subscribe to WWW.CARRIECSTONE.COM for my latest blogs and schedule of upcoming events. There you'll also find a forum where you can share your battles and your victories with me and others as you fight fear and win!

To arrange a speaking engagement with Carrie C. Stone,
please contact:
1-877-221-8564